CARLO SCARPA

Text by Sergio Los
Photographs by Klaus Frahm

CARLO SCARPA

Benedikt Taschen

© 1993 Benedikt Taschen Verlag GmbH
Hohenzollernring 53, D-50672 Köln
© 1993 Archivio Carlo Scarpa, Tobia Scarpa, Trevignano

Bildredaktion, Gestaltung, Produktion: Gabriele Leuthäuser, Nürnberg
Lektorat: Barbro Garenfeld Büning, Köln
Umschlag: Udo Bernstein, Nürnberg
Übersetzung ins Deutsche: Brigitte Brinkmann-Siepmann, Tübingen
Übersetzung ins Englische: John S. Scott, Garmisch-Partenkirchen
Übersetzung ins Französische: Marie-Anne Trémeau-Böhm, Köln
Satz: Utesch Satztechnik GmbH, Hamburg
Reproduktionen: NUREG, Nürnberg
Montage: Erwin Ratschmeier Montage-Service, Nürnberg

Printed in Italy
ISBN 3-8228-9441-9

CONTENTS

ESSAY CARLO SCARPA ARCHITECT

When I think of Carlo Scarpa as a teacher, the first thing I remember is that he was a rather shadowy figure in the Department. His presence was always felt, but he was seldom to be seen. He taught architectural drawing, and classes with him had to be arranged by phone either at his office or his home. He had few students, so I could spend whole afternoons alone with him. I came to realise that his drawings were very individual, a long way from simple utilitarian representations of existing or projected buildings. His teaching aimed at a form of drawing intended as thought. Thus, drawings for him were creative reflections, deliberations to explain something, or arguments which might be right or wrong and were thus far more than merely realistic depictions.

I grew up in Marostica, near Vicenza, and played as a child inside the castle walls, among the farmhouse porticos and on terraces held up by dry-stone walls, typical of areas of hillside cultivation, amidst a maze of vineyards and river embankments criss-crossed by trampled paths. I have always felt very drawn to this kind of construction, half building and half landscape. At that time the American Frank Lloyd Wright was the architect whose work I believed most closely reflected this interplay of building and natural environment. It seemed to me that he translated into architectural form my own somewhat confused feelings on this branch of human creativity.

When I arrived in Venice wishing to learn to build such houses, Scarpa seemed to be the architect whose works came nearest to Wright's. While attending two courses on interior design and architectural representation, I realised that for me Scarpa was far more than just an imparter of Wright's ideas. I realised that the connection between architecture and context was highly complex and that first and foremost the relationship with other buildings was of prime importance. I saw that behind the most remote houses was a town with a story to tell. After attending these two courses I became aware that on completing my studies I should try to join Scarpa's team.

THE CONTEXT

Who was Scarpa at that time? In what context had he developed his architecture? He had studied at the Academy of Fine Arts in Venice during the transition from Classicism to Secession. The exemplary work of Otto Wagner, the doyen of the Viennese school, drew Scarpa's attention to Josef Hoffmann and Charles Rennie Mackintosh, whose approach paid particular attention to tectonics, craftsmanship and material. Scarpa repeatedly mentioned that during his time at the Academy, more than at the Departments of Architecture, a craft atmosphere prevailed that was reminiscent

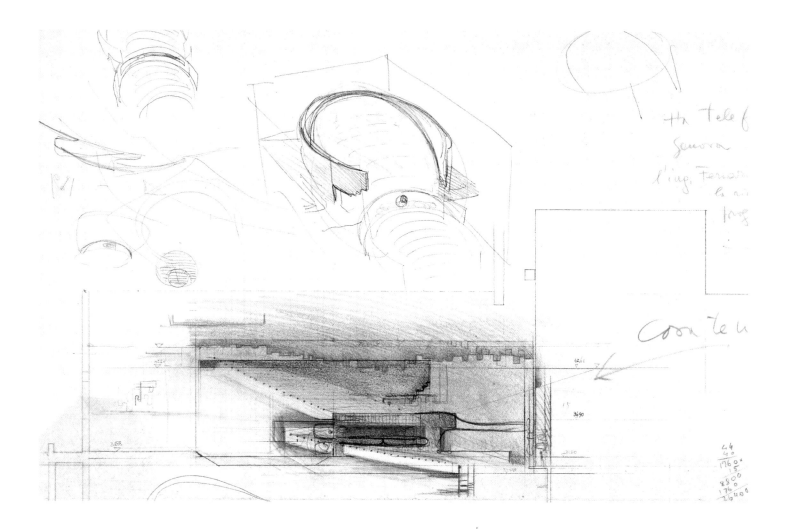

Wenn ich an Carlo Scarpa als Lehrer zurückdenke, so bleibt mir als erster Eindruck im Gedächtnis, daß er an der Fakultät auf geradezu geheimnisvolle Weise präsent war: Seine Anwesenheit war immer spürbar, aber man bekam ihn nur selten zu Gesicht. Er lehrte Architekturzeichnen, und der Unterricht fand bei Zusammenkünften statt, die man mit ihm telefonisch zu Hause oder in seinem Büro vereinbaren mußte. Er hatte nur wenige Studenten, so daß ich ganze Nachmittage mit ihm alleine verbringen konnte. Mit der Zeit wurde mir klar, daß Scarpa eine sehr eigenwillige Art zu zeichnen hatte, die nichts mehr mit einer schlichten, nur auf den praktischen Zweck ausgerichteten Darstellung bereits existierender oder geplanter Bauwerke zu tun hatte. Sein Unterricht zielte vielmehr auf ein Zeichnen ab, das sich als Denken verstand. Die Zeichnungen wurden daher bei ihm zu schöpferischen Reflexionen, zu Überlegungen, die etwas erklären sollten, zu Argumentationen, die richtig oder falsch sein konnten und daher mehr waren als lediglich mehr oder weniger realistische Darstellungen.

Ich bin in Marostica, in der Nähe von Vicenza, aufgewachsen und habe dort als Kind innerhalb der Burgmauern gespielt, zwischen den Schuppen der Bauernhäuser, den Terrassen, die, typisch für den Anbau am Hang, von Trockenmauern abgestützt waren, inmitten

Quand je songe à Carlo Scarpa comme professeur, ma première impression est que sa présence à la faculté était franchement mystérieuse: elle était toujours sensible, mais on le voyait rarement. Il enseignait le dessin d'architecture, et les cours avaient lieu pendant des réunions qu'il fallait fixer avec lui par téléphone, soit chez lui soit dans son bureau. Il avait seulement quelques étudiants, si bien que j'ai pu passer des après-midi entiers, seul avec lui. Avec le temps, j'ai compris que Scarpa avait une manière bien à lui de dessiner qui n'avait plus rien à voir avec la simple représentation de bâtiments existants ou en projet; elle était uniquement orientée vers le but pratique. Son enseignement visait au contraire un dessin conçu comme une réflexion. Les dessins devenaient donc chez lui des réflexions créatrices, des raisonnements qui devaient expliquer quelque chose, des argumentations qui pouvaient être justes ou fausses et étaient donc davantage que des représentations plus ou moins réalistes.

J'ai grandi à Marostica, près de Vicence et y ai joué, enfant, à l'intérieur des murs du château, entre les hangars des fermes et les terrasses étayées par des murs en pierres sèches typiques des cultures étagées, au milieu des vignes, le long des digues fluviales bordées de sentiers battus. J'ai toujours été vivement attiré par ce genre d'édifices, à la fois construction et paysage. A

Brion Family Cemetery, San Vito d'Altivole,
1969–1978; sketches for a gate

of a building-site. It should be mentioned that unlike other contemporary architects, such as Ludwig Mies van der Rohe, Scarpa came into modern architecture via the Secession – the movement known in the English-speaking world as Art nouveau – and not via Neoclassicism. This point of departure was decisive for the evolution of that particular Modernist architectural language. The ideas underlying the work of Modernists from Claude-Nicolas Ledoux to Le Corbusier had meant the severance of architectural composition from the visual tradition which linked architecture with the other visual arts. The distinction between design and construction made it possible to produce a kind of drawing able to depict not only facts but also wishes, not only the present but also the future. Drawing became the common »writing« of a »figurative language« of form in the early Renaissance, which embraced painting, sculpture and architecture as well. In my opinion, all attempts to separate architecture from the other visual arts and raise it to the status of an independent discipline lead only to design becoming a matter of calculation and technical craftsmanship instead of art. Pictorial thinking, thinking in images, which distinguishes Scarpa's approach, is part of a tradition which goes beyond the handicraft and even withstands the mathematical approach of engineers.

Scarpa said: »I draw because I want to see.« This shows the extent of the connection between seeing and knowing in his mind. It means that an architectural design proceeds from this differentiation between drawing and construction, which makes craft skills a topic of debate while preventing a descent to mere calculation, which came in with the architecture of the Enlightenment when architectural treatises became nothing but technical manuals.

Scarpa always distanced himself from the functionalist as well as the historical schematism of the modern

des Geflechts der Weinberge, an den von Trampelpfaden durchzogenen Dämmen des Flusses. Ich habe mich stets sehr angezogen gefühlt von dieser Art Bauwerke, die Konstruktion und Landschaft zugleich waren. Der Amerikaner Frank Lloyd Wright war damals derjenige Architekt, von dem ich den Eindruck hatte, daß er in seiner Arbeit auf dieses Zusammenspiel von Gebäude und natürlicher Umgebung am ehesten einging. Mir schien, daß er meine eigenen, eher intuitiven Überlegungen zu dieser Gestaltungsarbeit des Menschen in die Architektur umsetzte.

Als ich nach Venedig kam, mit dem Wunsch, dort zu lernen, wie man solche Häuser baut, galt Scarpa als derjenige, der mit seinen architektonischen Kompositionen Wright am nächsten kam. Im Verlauf zweier Kurse, die ich bei ihm belegte – Innenarchitektur und Architekturzeichnen, verbunden mit darstellender Geometrie –, wurde mir jedoch klar, daß Scarpa sehr viel mehr für mich bedeutete als nur ein Vermittler der Architektur Wrights. Ich begriff, daß das Verhältnis von Architektur und Landschaft äußerst komplex war, daß dabei immer und vorrangig die Beziehungen zu anderen Gebäuden ausschlaggebend waren, daß auch hinter den entlegensten Häusern immer eine Stadt mit einer Geschichte zu finden war. Am Ende dieser beiden Kurse stand für mich fest, daß ich unmittelbar nach Abschluß meines Studiums versuchen sollte, in Scarpas Architekturbüro einzutreten.

DER KONTEXT

Wer war Scarpa zu diesem Zeitpunkt? In welchem Kontext hatte sich seine Architektur entwickelt? Sein Studium an der Accademia di Belle Arti in Venedig hatte in einem Klima des Übergangs vom Klassizismus zur Sezession stattgefunden. Die exemplarische Entwicklung Otto Wagners, dem Nestor der Wiener Moderne, lenkte Scarpas Aufmerksamkeit auf Josef Hoffmann und Charles Rennie Mackintosh, die in ihrer Architektur besonderen Wert auf die tektonischen Aspekte, auf das Handwerkliche und auf die Materialien legten. Scarpa erwähnte immer wieder, daß damals, mehr als an den Architekturfakultäten, an der Akademie eine Art handwerkliche Atmosphäre geherrscht habe, die an eine Baustelle erinnerte. Man muß wissen, daß Scarpa im Unterschied zu anderen zeitgenössischen Architekten wie etwa Ludwig Mies van der Rohe über die Sezession, also jene Bewegung, die in Deutschland als Jugendstil bekannt wurde, und nicht über den Neoklassizismus zur modernen Architektur gekommen war. Dieser Ausgangspunkt war ganz entscheidend für die Herausbildung der sehr individuellen modernen Architektursprache, die Scarpa für die Komposition seiner Werke verwendete. Der Gedanke, der dem Projekt der Moderne von Claude-Nicolas Ledoux bis zu Le Corbu-

l'époque, l'Américain Frank Lloyd Wright était l'architecte qui, à mon avis, se prêtait le mieux à ce jeu du bâtiment et de l'environnement naturel dans son travail. J'avais l'impression qu'il convertissait en architecture mes propres réflexions plutôt intuitives à propos du travail créateur de l'homme.

Quand j'arrivai à Venise, désireux d'y apprendre comment on construit de telles maisons, Scarpa passait pour la personne la plus proche de Wright à cause de ses compositions architectoniques. Je m'inscrivis à deux de ses cours – décoration d'intérieurs et dessin d'architecture en rapport avec la géométrie descriptive – toutefois, je me rendis compte que Scarpa représentait beaucoup plus qu'un simple intermédiaire entre l'architecture de Wright et moi. Je compris que la relation entre l'architecture et le paysage était extrêmement complexe, que les rapports avec les autres bâtiments étaient toujours et avant tout décisifs, et qu'il y avait toujours une ville avec une histoire derrière les maisons les plus isolées. A la fin de ces deux cours, il était clair que je devais essayer d'entrer dans l'agence de Scarpa dès que j'aurais terminé mes études.

LE CONTEXTE

Qui était Scarpa à cette époque? Dans quel contexte son architecture s'était-elle développée? Ses études à l'Academia di Belle Arti à Venise s'étaient déroulées dans l'ambiance du passage du Classicisme à la Sécession. L'évolution exemplaire d'Otto Wagner, pionnier du Moderne viennois, attira l'attention de Scarpa sur Josef Hoffmann et Charles Rennie Mackintosh, qui donnait dans son architecture une grande place aux aspects tectoniques, à l'artisanat et aux matériaux. Scarpa répétait toujours que, bien plus que dans les facultés d'architecture, il régnait alors à l'académie une sorte d'atmosphère artisanale qui rappelait celle d'un chantier. Il faut savoir que, contrairement aux autres architectes contemporains tels que Ludwig Mies van der Rohe, Scarpa était parvenu à l'architecture moderne par l'intermédiaire de la Sécession, mouvement connu en Allemagne sous le nom de «Jugendstil», et non par l'intermédiaire du Néo-classicisme. Ce point de départ fut décisif pour la formation du langage architectonique moderne tout à fait individuel que Scarpa employait pour composer ses œuvres. La pensée, qui était à la base du projet moderne depuis Claude-Nicolas Ledoux jusqu'à Le Corbusier, avait entraîné la séparation entre la création architectonique et la tradition visuelle, qui rangeait l'architecture avec les autres arts plastiques. La distinction entre le dessin et la construction rendit possible une sorte de projet, qui était en mesure de rendre non seulement les faits mais aussi les désirs, non seulement le présent mais aussi le futur. Le dessin devint donc l'«écriture» commune d'un langage

Carlo Scarpa and Sergio Los

school. His feeling for learning by doing protected him from their abstractions. On the other hand, his profound historical knowledge enabled him to avoid both stylistically vague illustrations as well as the search for a »Zeitgeist« to legitimise the overthrow of natural architectural language. His cultivated perception is so rich that no-one could think it is based only on visual experience. The complexity of his outlook, where one image refers always to another, does not allow one to attribute it to the psychology of visual perception. Scarpa's ability to create designs with their own visual logic, based on a profound knowledge of traditional shapes which supplied him with the criteria of selection and evaluation, is a kind of »linguistic« competence. This sort of competence, formulated and developed by the artist-builders of the early Renaissance, later came to be regarded as mere theatricality, having been superseded by the scientific idea of objectivity.

As the classico-baroque gave way to the Secession style, there was a gradual transition from figure to form. If one studies the transition from the late baroque to the »pavilion system« that was considered by Giedion and Kaufmann to identify the architecture of the Enlightenment, one appreciates Scarpa's talent. Scarpa never used analytical architecture based on a juxtaposition of geometrically defined volumes. He accepted a Neo-Plasticist decomposition of space without passing through Neoclassicism. Through his figures he gradually achieved a transition to the pure forms of modern abstraction.

Scarpa's first drawings, apart from his student work, were in the language of Neo-Plasticism which he derived from Frank Lloyd Wright. But one must note the differences: what fascinated Scarpa about this architectural language was not the deconstruction of space in imaginary surfaces but rather the possibility of discovering joints to reconstitute the whole.

It is interesting to compare Scarpa's attitude to the new spatial concept of Neo-Plasticism with that of other architects. Two of them, Richard Neutra and Rudolph Schindler, who belonged to his generation, both from the Wagner school, with their Vienna background and attention to detail, are close to Scarpa though they were nearer to Frank Lloyd Wright in terms of culture than to Mies van der Rohe, for example. Although coming from Wagner they nonetheless radically restructured his architectural outlook, if maintaining his eye for detail and his feeling for the significance of materials. But by saying this I would not wish to imply that Scarpa's architectural outlook resembled Neutra's or Schindler's, I mean only that he came upon the discovery of the new space by a similar path.

Frank Lloyd Wright's work had interested Scarpa for years and he had tried to imagine it from publications,

sier zugrunde lag, hatte die Trennung der architektonischen Gestaltung von jener visuellen Tradition bedeutet, die die Architektur mit den anderen bildenden Künsten zusammensah. Die Unterscheidung von Zeichnung und Konstruktion ermöglichte eine Art des Entwurfs, der nicht nur die Fakten, sondern auch die Wünsche, nicht nur die Gegenwart, sondern auch die Zukunft wiederzugeben in der Lage war. Die Zeichnung wurde so zur gemeinsamen »Schrift« einer Formensprache, die sich in der Frührenaissance herausgebildet hatte und sowohl Malerei als auch Skulptur und Architektur umfaßte. Meines Erachtens führen alle Versuche, die Architektur aus ihrer Verbundenheit mit den anderen bildenden Künsten herauszulösen, um ihr den Anspruch einer unabhängigen Disziplin zu verschaffen, nur dazu, daß im Entwurf an die Stelle der Zeichnung die Berechnung und das rein technische Handwerk treten. Das bildnerische Denken, das Denken in Figuren, das die Sichtweise Scarpas auszeichnete, gehört in eine Tradition, die über das rein Handwerkliche hinausgeht und zugleich der Mathematisierung durch den Ingenieur widersteht.

Scarpa sagte: »Ich zeichne, weil ich sehen will.« Das macht deutlich, in welchem Maße für ihn Sehen mit Erkennen zu tun hatte. Es bedeutet, daß der architektonische Entwurf sich aus jener Unterscheidung von Zeichnung und Konstruktion ergibt, die das rein handwerkliche Können problematisiert und andererseits zugleich die Reduktion auf die reine Berechnung verhindert, die mit der Architektur der Aufklärung eingesetzt hatte, als die architektonischen Abhandlungen zu puren Handbüchern wurden.

Scarpa hatte sich immer vom funktionalistischen und historistischen Schematismus der Moderne ferngehalten: Sein Sinn für das »Erkennen durch Tun« bewahrte ihn vor der Abstraktheit der Blockdiagramme, die an die Stelle der distributiven Merkmale des Typus traten, um auf diese Weise eine im Hinblick auf die Architektur neutrale topologische Metasprache zu erreichen. Auf der anderen Seite ermöglichte ihm seine profunde Kenntnis der Geschichte, sowohl stilistisch unbestimmte Darstellungen zu vermeiden als auch sich der Suche nach jenem »Zeitgeist« zu entziehen, der die Überwindung der natürlichen Architektursprachen legitimieren sollte.

Sein von kulturellem Wissen geprägter Blick ist frei von dem Verdacht, bloße Wahrnehmungserfahrung zu sein. Die Komplexität seiner Sichtweise, bei der ein Bild immer auf andere Bilder verweist, schließt jede schnelle Reduktion auf die Wahrnehmungspsychologie aus. Scarpas Fähigkeit, die gezeichneten Formfiguren dieser visuellen Logik entsprechend zu handhaben – angeleitet von einer profunden Kenntnis der Tradition der Formensprache, welche ihm die Kriterien für Be-

formel, qui s'était établi au début de la Renaissance et comprenait aussi bien la peinture que la sculpture et l'architecture. A mon avis, toutes les tentatives entreprises pour libérer l'architecture de son attachement aux autres arts plastiques, afin de lui donner le rang de discipline autonome, aboutissent seulement à ce que le calcul et l'artisanat purement technique remplacent le dessin dans le projet. La pensée créatrice, la pensée figurée qui caractérise la manière de voir de Scarpa, fait partie d'une tradition, qui va au-delà de l'artisanat pur et s'oppose en même temps à ce que l'ingénieur la transforme en mathématiques.

Scarpa a dit un jour: «Je dessine parce que je veux voir». Cela montre clairement dans quelle mesure la vue et la connaissance sont liées pour lui. Cela signifie que le projet architectonique résulte de la distinction entre le dessin et la construction, qui pose le problème du savoir-faire purement artisanal et empêche par contre en même temps la réduction à un pur calcul, qui avait commencé avec l'architecture de l'«Aufklärung», époque à laquelle les thèses architectoniques devinrent de purs manuels.

Scarpa s'était toujours tenu à l'écart du schématisme fonctionnaliste et historiciste du Moderne: son sens pour reconnaître-en-faisant le préservait de l'abstraction des schémas fonctionnels, qui prenaient la place des caractéristiques distributives du type, pour parvenir de cette manière à un métalangage topologique neutre au niveau de l'architecture. D'autre part, sa profonde connaissance de l'histoire lui permettait non seulement d'éviter les représentations indéterminées quant au style, mais aussi de se soustraire à la recherche de l'«esprit du siècle», qui devait légitimer le triomphe remporté sur les langages architectoniques naturels.

Son regard marqué par la culture ne peut être soupçonné d'être une simple expérience basée sur la perception. La complexité de sa manière de voir, dans laquelle une image renvoie toujours à d'autres images, exclut toute réduction rapide à la psychologie de la perception. Scarpa était capable de se servir des figures formelles dessinées conformément à cette logique visuelle – guidée par une profonde connaissance de la tradition du langage formel, qui lui donnait les critères nécessaires pour noter et choisir la figure formelle chaque fois appropriée –; c'est là une compétence «linguistique» de par son essence. C'est une compétence que les artistes-bâtisseurs du début de la Renaissance avaient développée et mise en théorie, mais qui fut par la suite supplantée par l'idéal objectif des sciences naturelles, parce qu'elle était seulement considérée comme un simple «effet théâtral».

Au fur et à mesure que le système architectonique classico-baroque faisait place à celui de la Sécession, on assista également à un passage progressif de la figure à

Brion Family Cemetery, San Vito d'Altivole,
1969–1978; view and section of the chapel,
from the north-west

but when at the end of the sixties he was able to see it at first hand he was disappointed by the absence of structural details which, he thought, distinguished the new architecture. Scarpa's own formal language had attained self-sufficiency in these years, and architecture was in a state of radical change which alienated it from Wright's legacy.

Louis Kahn was developing his »architecture of remembrance«, which was closely related to Scarpa's design outlook in its attention to details and to joints. Kahn asserted that the joint was at the origin of ornament.

When Scarpa applied the Neo-Plasticist decomposition of space, he considered not surfaces but structural joints. Instead of formulating a repertory of rectangular areas

wertung und Auswahl der jeweils richtigen Formfigur an die Hand gab –, diese Fähigkeit Scarpas ist eine ihrem Wesen nach »linguistische« Kompetenz. Es ist eine Kompetenz, die die Künstler-Baumeister der Frührenaissance entwickelt und theoretisiert hatten, die aber dann durch das Objektivitätsideal der Naturwissenschaften verdrängt wurde, weil sie für bloßen »Bühnenzauber« gehalten wurde.

Mit der Entwicklung vom klassisch-barocken Architektursystem zu dem der Sezession vollzog sich auch der schrittweise Übergang von der Figur zur Form. Verfolgt man den Prozeß vom Spätbarock zum »pavillon system«, das nach Ansicht von Giedion und Kaufmann die Architektur der Aufklärung kennzeichnet, dann er-

la forme. Si l'on suit le processus de la fin du Baroque au «pavillon system», qui caractérise pour Giedion et Kaufmann l'architecture de l'«Aufklärung», on saisit alors le caractère exceptionnel de Scarpa. Scarpa n'est jamais parvenu au langage architectonique analytique, qui résulte de la juxtaposition de volumes de construction définis par la géométrie. Son chemin l'a au contraire conduit à la décomposition néo-plastique de l'espace, sans toutefois passer par le Néo-classicisme. Dans ses figures formelles, il est peu à peu passé aux formes pures de l'abstraction moderne.

Si l'on excepte les travaux d'étude réalisés par Scarpa à l'académie, ses premiers dessins se sont exercés dans le langage d'un Néo-plasticisme qui émanait de Wright. Il

Book Pavilion at the Venice Biennale, 1950
(above); installations for the Venice Biennale,
1952 (centre and below)

without stipulating their location (floor, wall, ceiling) and thus attaining the abstraction of the Dutch De Stijl, Scarpa stressed the joints and sought to enhance them by dissociating the whole into its component parts. With Scarpa this dissociation was not an intentional breach of the rules, but it was the only way he could introduce the joints which justified ornamentation without turning his back on the modern movement.[1]

Scarpa knew how much the loss of ornament – showing, at the joints, what the compositional elements are doing – would stultify architecture. Profiles, edges, mouldings etc. show how the elements of a building attack and repel each other, while their disappearance leaves all relations between these elements in limbo. Scarpa's designs were intended to supersede all these ancient architectural »prepositions«.

DETAIL AND CRAFTSMANSHIP

Scarpa did not believe that the realisation of architectural images by stonemasons, carpenters and the like should be limited to the mere execution of a drawing, because for him it also involved creative contemplation, a permanent source of inspiration for the design of his unusual details. Exhaustive discussions with the manual workers bear witness to this exchange of knowledge and to the constructive craft basis which accompanied the finalizing of much of Scarpa's work, helping to develop his architectural language.

His draft design provided the productive exchange with a script; it provided the craftsmen with a score, a system of notation. For Scarpa, draughtsmanship was comparable to the virtuosity of a performing musician: it demanded the same visual control. The drawing followed its own tradition; it too had its marks of virtuosity, its technique of instrumentation.

Scarpa's decomposition of space was determined by the progress of the building work. The »cut« of the various elements was a product of the site context, even when the work was carried out by different craftsmen. In his first attempts at the architecture of decomposition, his »fragments« can be taken as episodes of construction. The first step in the development of his architecture thus created a union between workshop and Academy, ending a separation between craftsmanship and the academic approach which had begun with the first working drawings. Hence, in my opinion, a technical interpretation of Scarpa's designs is more appropriate than the usual highly formal approach.

The Secession school, through the Venice Biennale, had influenced the Venetian visual arts since the end of the First World War, finding there an environment highly favourable to local artistic traditions. The many carpenters, stone masons, glaziers, plasterers etc. who made up the highly valued local building trade were

faßt man auch die Besonderheit Scarpas, denn Scarpa gelangte nie zu jener analytischen Architektursprache, die sich aus der Juxtaposition von geometrisch definierten Bauvolumina ergibt. Sein Weg führte ihn vielmehr zur neoplastischen Dekomposition des Raums, ohne jedoch durch den Neoklassizismus hindurchgegangen zu sein. In seinen Formfiguren fand er ganz allmählich den Übergang zu den reinen Formen der modernen Abstraktion.

Scarpas erste Zeichnungen – läßt man seine Studienarbeiten an der Akademie beiseite – übten sich in der Sprache eines Neoplastizismus, der sich von Wright herleitete. Man muß jedoch die Unterschiede sehen: Was Scarpa an dieser Architektursprache faszinierte, war nicht die Dekonstruktion des Raumvolumens in imaginäre Flächen, als vielmehr die Möglichkeit, Punkte der Verknüpfung zu erfinden, die den Raum wieder zusammenfügten.

Es erscheint mir durchaus interessant, Scarpas Verhältnis zur neuen Raumauffassung des Neoplastizismus mit dem anderer Architekten zu vergleichen, die zwar zur selben Generation gehörten, sich aber in einem anderen kulturellen Ambiente bewegten, das Wright sehr viel näher war als beispielsweise Mies van der Rohe. Ich denke da an Richard Neutra und Rudolph Schindler, die mit ihrer Wiener Ausbildung und ihrer Sorgfalt bei der Ausführung von Details mit Scarpa zu vergleichen sind. Beide kamen aus der Schule Wagners, unterzogen seine Architektur jedoch einer radikalen Umgestaltung, bei der freilich weder der Sinn fürs Detail noch das Bewußtsein für die Bedeutung der Materialien verlorenging. Ich will damit keineswegs behaupten, daß Scarpas Architektur Ähnlichkeit mit der von Neutra und Schindler hat, ich meine nur, daß Scarpa auf einem analogen Weg zur Entdeckung des neuen Raums gelangte.

Als Scarpa Ende der sechziger Jahre die Möglichkeit erhielt, die Architektur von Wright, mit der er sich so lange beschäftigt hatte und die er sich anhand von Publikationen vorzustellen versuchte, vor Ort kennenzulernen, war er enttäuscht von ihrem Mangel an konstruktiven Einzelelementen, die er doch eigentlich für kennzeichnend hielt. Scarpas Formensprache hatte in diesen Jahren eine ihr eigene Selbständigkeit erlangt, und auch die Architekturszene befand sich in einem Umbruch, der sie dem Erbe Wrights entfremdete. Louis Kahn war dabei, eine »Architektur der Erinnerung« zu entwickeln, die Scarpas Gestaltungsabsichten sehr verwandt war, auch was ihre Aufmerksamkeit für die Punkte der Verknüpfung und für die Details betraf. Kahn behauptete: »Die Verknüpfung ist der Ursprung des Ornaments.«

Als Scarpa die neoplastizistische Dekomposition des Raums anwendete, richtete sich sein Augenmerk nicht

faut toutefois voir les différences: ce qui fascinait Scarpa dans ce langage architectonique, n'était pas la décomposition du volume spatial en surfaces imaginaires, mais au contraire la possibilité d'inventer des points d'attache, qui assemblaient de nouveau l'espace.

Il me semble fort intéressant de comparer les rapports de Scarpa et de la nouvelle conception spatiale du Néo-plasticisme avec ceux d'autres architectes, qui appartenaient à la même génération, mais se mouvaient dans un autre milieu culturel beaucoup plus proche de Wright que de Mies van der Rohe par exemple. Je pense à Richard Neutra et à Rudolph Schindler, que l'on peut comparer à Scarpa du fait de leur formation viennoise et des soins qu'ils apportaient à l'exécution des détails. Tous deux venaient de l'école de Wagner, mais soumirent son architecture à une transformation radicale au cours de laquelle, il est vrai, ni le sens du détail ni la conscience de l'importance des matériaux ne furent perdus. Je ne veux nullement affirmer que l'architecture de Scarpa ressemble à celle de Neutra et de Schindler, je pense seulement que Scarpa est parvenu d'une manière analogue à la découverte du nouvel espace.

Quand Scarpa eut l'occasion, à la fin des années soixante, de découvrir sur place l'architecture de Wright qui l'avait si longtemps occupé et qu'il essayait de s'imaginer à l'aide de publications, il fut déçu par son manque d'éléments individuels constructifs qu'il croyait pourtant caractéristiques. Au cours de ces années, le langage formel de Scarpa avait acquis son indépendance, et la scène architecturale était aussi plongée dans une révolution qui l'éloignait de l'héritage de Wright. Louis Kahn était en train de développer une «architecture du souvenir» qui était très proche des intentions créatrices de Scarpa, de même en ce qui concerne son attention pour les points d'attache et les détails. Kahn affirmait: «La liaison est l'origine de l'ornement». Quand Scarpa appliquait la décomposition néo-plastique de l'espace, il ne considérait pas les surfaces, mais leurs liaisons, les points d'articulation structurels. Au lieu de formuler un répertoire de surfaces rectangulaires, sans qualification détaillée de leur emplacement syntactique – sol, mur, plafond –, pour parvenir de cette façon à une abstraction radicale comme dans le mouvement néerlandais De Stijl, Scarpa mit l'accent sur les points de fixation et visa sa revalorisation en dissociant le tout en éléments individuels. Cette dissociation n'avait pas chez lui un caractère d'infraction aux règles, elle représentait au contraire l'unique possibilité d'introduire le point d'attache qui permettait l'ornement, sans tourner alors le dos au Moderne.[1] Scarpa savait dans quelle mesure la perte de l'ornement – qui montre ce que les éléments de composition

auf die Flächen, sondern auf ihre Verknüpfungen, die strukturellen Gelenkstellen. Statt ein Repertoire an rechtwinkligen Flächen zu formulieren, ohne jede nähere Qualifizierung ihres syntaktischen Standortes – Fußboden, Wand, Decke –, um auf diese Weise wie beim niederländischen De Stijl eine radikale Abstraktion zu erreichen, legte Scarpa den Akzent auf die Punkte ihrer Verklammerung und bezweckte mit der Dissoziation des Ganzen in Einzelelemente ihre Aufwertung. Diese Dissoziation hatte bei ihm nicht den Charakter eines Regelverstoßes, sie stellt vielmehr die einzige Möglichkeit dar, eben jene Stelle der Verknüpfung einzuführen, die das Ornament zuließ, ohne damit der Moderne den Rücken zu kehren.[1]

Mit diesen »Präpositionen« zum Raum bewahrte Scarpa den figurativen Charakter der antiken Baukunst mit Hilfe von Formfiguren, die einer »modernen« Natur entstammten. Statt Blattwerk und Blüten gaben seine Verknüpfungen Elemente der raffiniertesten Technologie, der Präzisionsinstrumente, der Photoapparate, der Meßgeräte etc. wieder.

Scarpa wußte, in welchem Maße der Verlust des Ornaments – das an den Verknüpfungspunkten das zeigt, was die kompositorischen Elemente »tun« – die Architektur zur Stummheit verurteilt. Profile, Lisenen, Bandgesimse, Zacken etc. zeigen an, wie die Komponenten eines Gebäudes sich attackieren, sich abstoßen, sich zwingen: Ihr Verschwinden dagegen läßt alle Beziehungen dieser Komponenten untereinander im Unbestimmten. Die von Scarpa gezeichneten Details sollten an die Stelle all jener antiken architektonischen »Präpositionen« treten.

DETAIL UND HANDWERK

Die Verwendung der architektonischen Figuren nach Maßgabe einer bauhandwerklichen Kompetenz beschränkte sich nach Auffassung Scarpas nicht einfach darauf, eine Form umzusetzen, einen zeichnerischen Entwurf auszuführen, sondern bedeutete die Ausübung einer schöpferischen Reflexion, die ihm beständige Quelle für die Entwürfe seiner ungewöhnlichen Details war. Die ausführlichen Gespräche mit den Handwerkern, die die Entwicklung und endgültige Festlegung vieler Episoden der Architektur Scarpas begleiteten, bezeugen diesen Austausch von Wissen und die konstruktive, bauhandwerkliche Basis, von der aus sich die Syntax seiner Architektursprache entwickelte.

Der zeichnerische Entwurf lieferte dieser produktiven Reflexion der Handarbeit eine Schrift, den Motiven des Handwerkers stellte sie eine Partitur, ein Notationssystem bereit. Für Scarpa war die Praxis des zeichnerischen Entwerfens vergleichbar mit der Meisterschaft des musikalischen Interpreten. Sie verlangte die gleiche manuelle Geschicklichkeit und wurde von einer analo-

«font» aux points d'attache – condamne l'architecture à être muette. Les profils, les lisières, les corniches en forme de bandes, les dents, etc. montrent comment les composantes d'un bâtiment s'attaquent, se repoussent, se forcent; leur disparition laisse par contre tous les rapports de ces composantes entre elles dans le vague. Les détails dessinés par Scarpa devaient remplacer toutes les «prépositions» architectoniques antiques.

DETAIL ET ARTISANAT

Selon Scarpa, l'emploi de figures architectoniques suivant une compétence artisanale ne se limitait pas simplement à convertir une forme, à réaliser un dessin; il impliquait au contraire une réflexion créatrice qui était pour lui une source permanente pour les dessins de ses extraordinaires détails. Les longs entretiens avec les artisans, qui accompagnaient le développement et la fixation définitive des nombreux épisodes de l'architecture de Scarpa, témoignent de cet échange de connaissances et de la base constructive et artisanale à partir de laquelle se développait la syntaxe de son langage architectural.

Le dessin fournissait à cette réflexion productive du travail manuel une écriture, elle fournissait aux motifs de l'artisan une partition, une notation. Pour Scarpa, la pratique du dessin était comparable à la perfection de l'interprète musical. Elle exigeait la même dextérité et était accompagnée d'un contrôle visuel analogue. Le dessin suivait aussi les motifs de la tradition, il possédait aussi ses formes de virtuosité et sa propre instrumentation.

La décomposition de l'espace de Scarpa était donc déterminée par le cours de la construction; la coupe des parties était le résultat de l'enchaînement du travail, même s'il était exécuté par divers artisans. A la base de son architecture de la décomposition, ses «fragments» se conçoivent comme épisodes de construction. Le premier pas vers le développement de son architecture réunit donc de nouveau l'artisanat et l'atelier avec l'académie, qui s'étaient éloignés l'un de l'autre depuis que le dessin et la construction avaient été séparés. C'est pourquoi, il me semble plus approprié de donner une interprétation technique et tectonique du dessin de Scarpa plutôt que d'en faire une interprétation habituelle souvent formaliste.

La Sécession, qui exerçait depuis la fin de la Première Guerre mondiale son influence sur les arts plastiques à Venise par l'intermédiaire de la Biennale, y rencontra une atmosphère tout à fait favorable à la grande tradition artisanale locale. Les nombreux menuisiers, marbriers, verriers, serruriers, stucateurs etc., qui représentent l'entreprise de construction composite, connurent une revalorisation sensible dans les articulations créatrices de l'architecture sécessionniste. Son sens des ma-

Gavina Showroom, Bologna, 1961–1963; detail
of a built-in fitting

Previous picture page: Banca Popolare di Verona,
Verona, 1973–1981; detail of staff staircase

tériaux, la combinaison de textures transmise par de précieuses corniches, le soin apporté à la création des points d'attache, la forme raffinée des détails, tout cela renvoie à un savoir artisanal accompli qu'il faut non seulement connaître, mais aussi avoir à sa disposition. Scarpa ne se contentait pas d'utiliser les techniques artisanales disponibles, mais procédait aussi à des échanges communicatifs avec les exécutants, qui devaient réaliser ses projets, afin de déployer leur savoir-faire et d'intensifier en même temps leur créativité. Scarpa fit revivre une culture artisanale menacée de disparition en revalorisant ses produits avec un genre de projet, qui les actualisait et les intégrait dans l'architecture moderne. Il mit également en évidence des possibilités d'intervention dans la restructuration d'édifices existants, en conservant des formes de travail de matériaux entre-temps tombées en désuétude qui reliaient le nouveau avec l'architecture du passé.

Convaincu de la possibilité de connaissance contenue dans les façons de faire, dans la fabrication, Scarpa introduisit de nouveau dans la culture artisanale le facteur intellectuel qui avait marqué le dessin depuis le début de la Renaissance.[2] Scarpa renvoyait toujours à la notion de «verum ipsum factum» de Vico, c'est-à-dire à l'idée que l'on parvient à la vérité par l'activité manuelle, créatrice, c'est à dire une conception comparable aux raisonnements de la dialectique.

LA VISUALISATION

Quand je commençai mon apprentissage dans l'agence de Scarpa après mes études, son aptitude à penser tout en dessinant fut extraordinairement instructive pour moi. Je pus directement observer la manière dont ses idées s'élaboraient sur le papier. La liaison volontaire des figures formelles suivait une logique complètement différente de la logique habituelle, c'est-à-dire abstraite et dérivée du langage. Elle semblait au contraire guidée par une rationalité créatrice donnant lieu à des démarches qui semblaient apparemment inutiles ou trop naturelles, mais s'avéraient extrêmement productives l'instant d'après. Cette réflexion visuelle, qui s'accomplit dans le mode du dessin, caractérise donc aussi les formes de la référence, qui sont le point de départ du langage structurel de Scarpa. Elles sont en premier lieu exemplificatrices, même si elles conservent dans les détails le mode référentiel de la représentation figurée, de la citation, de l'expression. A l'université ou à l'agence, Scarpa recommandait fréquemment de se méfier de la représentation figurée dans le domaine de l'architecture. «Quand la forme que tu dessines a une quelconque ressemblance avec quoi que ce soit», disait-il, «alors efface-la.»

Comme la plupart des représentants de l'architecture abstraite, Scarpa pensait que les formes n'ont pas de

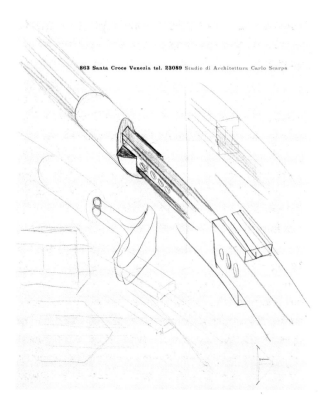

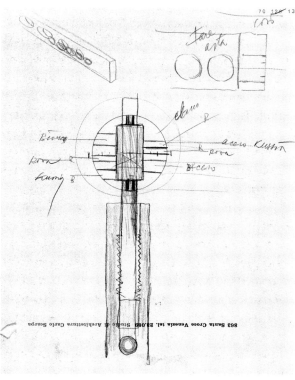

Brion Family Cemetery, San Vito d'Altivole,
1969–1978; sketches for linking elements

given a great boost to their prestige by the decorative innovations of Secession architecture. Their feeling for materials, the combination of textures put across by their cornices, the care they took in their joints, their clever details, all indicate a consummate skill which one feels impelled to use upon learning of it.

Scarpa did not restrict himself to using the available skills, but cultivated communication with the people who were to implement his drawings, developing both their skills and their creativity. He thus revived an artisan culture which had been threatened with disappearance. He enhanced it by designs which made the culture relevant, integrating it with contemporary architecture. Moreover, he showed that one could restructure existing buildings by employing almost-forgotten techniques which provided a link between the new and the old.

With his conviction that one can learn by doing, Scarpa also developed the intellectual side of manual work which had typified mechanical drawing since the early Renaissance.[2] Following Giovanni Battista Vico's maxim, »verum ipsum factum«, Scarpa emphasized that one reaches the truth through manual constructional work, a thought akin to the logic of dialectical reasoning.

VISUALISATION

When, after finishing my studies, I joined Scarpa's team as an apprentice, I found his ability to think while producing his drawings extraordinarily instructive. I was able to observe directly how his thoughts evolved on paper. His highly personal way of linking the various elements together followed a logic which was quite different from the normal conceptual logic of language. It seemed rather to derive from a figurative logic which demanded steps at first apparently unnecessary or obvious, but which then proved to be highly productive. This visual thinking which took place as the design was sketched out thus also characterized the modes of reference, the point of departure, for Scarpa's compositional language. They were primarily exemplifications, even when the details adhered to the referential mode of depiction, of quotation and of expression. Scarpa frequently warned his students and staff to distrust pictorial representation in architecture. He maintained that if what we were drawing resembled anything, then it should be erased.

Like most abstract architects, Scarpa was of the opinion that shapes have no associative or conventional meanings. Architectural forms, he thought, refer purely to themselves, and are based on a non-denotative referentiality, on exemplification.

That at least was the theory. But once its normative character had begun to wear off, Scarpa was free to

gen visuellen Kontrolle begleitet. Auch der zeichnerische Entwurf folgte den Motiven der eigenen Tradition, auch er besaß seine Formen der Virtuosität und eine eigene Instrumentierung.

Scarpas Dekomposition des Raums wurde daher vom Gang der Konstruktion bestimmt, der Schnitt der Teile ergab sich aus dem Zusammenhang der Arbeit, auch wenn sie von verschiedenen Handwerkern ausgeführt wurde. Im ersten Ansatz seiner Architektur der Dekomposition verstehen sich seine »Fragmente« als Episoden der Konstruktion. Der erste Schritt in der Entwicklung seiner Architektur führte also Handwerk und Werkstatt wieder mit der Akademie zusammen, die sich seit der Trennung von zeichnerischem Entwurf und Konstruktion einander entfremdet hatten. Daher ist eine technisch-tektonische Interpretation des zeichnerischen Entwurfs von Carlo Scarpa meines Erachtens angemessener als die übliche, weitgehend formalistische Interpretation.

Die Sezession, die über die Biennale ihren Einfluß auf die bildenden Künste in Venedig seit dem Ende des Ersten Weltkriegs ausübte, traf dort auf ein Ambiente, das der großen lokalen Handwerkstradition durchaus günstig war. Die vielen Schreiner, Marmorsteinmetze, Glaser, Schlosser, Stukkateure u.a., die das vielfältig zusammengesetzte Bauunternehmen darstellen, erfuhren eine deutliche Aufwertung in den gestalterischen Artikulationen der sezessionistischen Architektur. Deren Sinn für die Materialien, die Kombination ihrer Texturen, vermittelt durch preziöse Gesimse, die Sorgfalt in der Gestaltung der Verknüpfungspunkte, die raffinierte Form der Details, all das verweist auf ein vollendetes Handwerkskönnen, das man nicht einfach nur kennen, sondern über das man ebenso verfügen muß. Scarpa beschränkte sich nicht darauf, die vorhandenen handwerklichen Fertigkeiten einzusetzen, er pflegte vielmehr den kommunikativen Austausch mit den Ausführenden, die seine Entwürfe realisieren sollten, um so ihr Können zur Entfaltung zu bringen und zugleich ihre Kreativität zu steigern. Scarpa ließ eine Handwerkskultur wiederaufleben, die verlorenzugehen drohte, weil er ihre Erzeugnisse mit einer Art des zeichnerischen Entwurfs aufwertete, der sie aktualisierte und in die Gegenwartsarchitektur integrierte. Zudem zeigte er Möglichkeiten auf, in die Umstrukturierung bereits Gebauten einzugreifen, indem er inzwischen ungebräuchlich gewordene Formen der Materialbearbeitung beibehielt, die das Neue mit der Architektur der Vergangenheit verbanden.

Mit seiner Überzeugung von der im Tun, im Herstellen enthaltenen Erkenntnismöglichkeit führt Scarpa wieder jenes intellektuelle Moment in die Handwerkskultur ein, das den zeichnerischen Entwurf seit der Frührenaissance geprägt hatte.[2] Scarpa verwies immer wieder

significations associatives et conventionnelles, que les formes architectoniques signifient seulement ce qu'elles sont, qu'elles se fondent sur une référence non dénotative, sur l'exemplification. Tel était son enseignement. Mais dès que leur importance normative diminuait, Scarpa pouvait facilement développer à fond la complexité référentielle de son architecture. Les nœuds et les points de Gottfried Semper, qu'il qualifia – avec la boiserie et le cannage – de point de départ fondamental de l'architecture, représentent les motifs qui permirent de surmonter une conception statique de représentation figurée et introduisirent une dimension programmatique et dynamique. Si la danse est le mode poétique de la marche, il existe alors aussi un savoirfaire du charpentier, du marbrier ou du tisserand qui métamorphose les motifs architectoniques en formes et en fait des modes poétiques de la construction. Si l'on considère cette conception dynamique et opérationnelle de représentation figurée comme point de départ matérialiste pour ce qui est de la théorie de l'architecture, cela signifie également l'abolition de la dimension référentielle et symbolique.

Alors que je préparais des notes de cours pour les étudiants dans les années soixante et que j'expliquais comment un projet naissait chez Scarpa par l'intermédiaire du dessin, je qualifiais cela de poétique.[3] Cet aspect est une autre justification du caractère non dénotatif de la référence structurelle du langage architectonique de Scarpa. C'est que le langage de la poésie est introverti, son contenu est «opaque» – les raisonnements intuitifs de Konrad Fiedler à propos de la nontransparence des arts plastiques sont tout à fait justes –, mais uniquement à cause de son caractère spécifiquement poétique et artistique, et non pas à cause de son caractère figuratif comme dans la psychologie de la perception.[4] Dans le langage poétique, la forme est si importante que sa distinction du contenu, auquel elle renvoie, est difficile, sinon impossible. Si on les considère sous cet angle, les œuvres de Scarpa ne semblent pas avoir d'autre contenu que leur forme. La référence exemplificatrice et le caractère poétique de leur communication cachent leur dimension textuelle. Les charnières et les liaisons de Scarpa, par exemple entre des colonnes géminées, exemplifient la technologie raffinée des appareils scientifiques, les coupes dans les panneaux et les dentelures exemplifient le miroir et la charpente de l'architecture classique. Elles ne reproduisent pas les technologies mécaniques d'une manière figurée, comme cela est le cas pour certaines transmissions techniques, pas davantage les profils de la structure architectonique comme dans le style historiciste. Les œuvres de Scarpa exemplifient les rythmes, les mouvements, les textures des référents, en ce sens qu'elles partagent avec eux ces qualités et montrent

Carlo Scarpa in his Vicenza office, 1972

auf Vicos Gedanken vom »verum ipsum factum«, auf jene Einsicht also, daß man über die manuelle, herstellende Tätigkeit zur Wahrheit gelange, ein Gedanke, der mit den logischen Überlegungen der dialektischen Argumentation vergleichbar ist.

DIE VISUALISIERUNG

Als ich nach Abschluß meines Studiums meine Lehrzeit in Scarpas Architekturbüro antrat, war seine Fähigkeit, im Vollzug des Zeichnens zu denken, für mich außerordentlich lehrreich. Ich konnte direkt beobachten, wie sich seine Gedanken auf dem Papier entwickelten. Die eigenwillige Verknüpfung der Formfiguren folgte einer Logik, die sich von der gewohnten, das heißt begrifflichen, von der Sprache herkommenden Logik völlig unterschied. Sie schien vielmehr angeleitet von einer bildnerischen Rationalität, die zu Schrittfolgen veranlaßte, die scheinbar unnötig oder allzu selbstverständlich schienen, die sich aber gleich darauf als äußerst produktiv erwiesen.

Dieses visuelle Denken, das sich im Modus des zeichnerischen Entwerfens vollzieht, kennzeichnet daher auch die Formen der Referenzialität, die Ausgangspunkt von Scarpas kompositorischer Sprache sind. Sie sind in erster Linie exemplifikatorisch, auch wenn sie in den Details den referentiellen Modus der bildlichen Darstellung, des Zitats, des Ausdrucks beibehalten. Scarpa ermahnte einen häufig, an der Universität oder im Büro, der bildlichen Darstellung in der Architektur zu mißtrauen. »Wenn sich in der Form, die du zeichnest, eine Ähnlichkeit mit irgend etwas zeigt«, sagte er, »dann radiere sie aus.«

Wie die meisten Vertreter der abstrakten Architektur war auch Scarpa der Auffassung, daß die Formen keine assoziativen, konventionellen Bedeutungen haben. Die Formen der Architektur bedeuteten lediglich sich selbst, sie gründeten auf einer nicht-denotativen Referenzialität, auf der Exemplifikation. So war die Lehre. Aber sobald deren normative Geltung nachließ, konnte Scarpa ungehindert die referentielle Komplexität seiner Architektur voll entwickeln.

Gottfried Sempers Knoten und Nähte, die er – zusammen mit der Täfelung und dem Flechtwerk – zum fundamentalen Ausgangspunkt der Architektur erklärte, stellen jene Motive dar, die die Überwindung einer statischen Auffassung von bildlicher Darstellung erlaubten und eine programmatische und dynamische Dimension einführten. Wenn das Tanzen der poetische Modus des Gehens ist, so gibt es ebenso ein Wissen des Zimmermanns, des Marmorsteinmetzen oder des Webers, das die Motive der Architektur in Formen umsetzt und sie zu poetischen Modi des Bauens werden läßt. Betrachtet man diese dynamische, operationale Konzeption von bildlicher Darstellung architekturtheore-

clairement leur importance. La recherche de Scarpa s'est dirigée vers un langage formel plus articulé et plus dense pour découvrir finalement que c'était un langage des figures.

Dans les travaux récents à propos de Scarpa, comme celui qu'a effectué Francesco Dal Co à l'occasion de l'exposition de 1984 à Venise, on essaie de mettre en évidence une nouvelle forme spécifique de référence dans les figures abstraites de l'architecture de Scarpa.[5] Les résultats de ces travaux sont confirmés par les nombreuses annotations dans les livres que la Signora Nini, veuve de Scarpa, a mis à notre disposition pour que nous les consultions, et que Scarpa avait apparemment examinés à diverses reprises. Je suis absolument d'accord avec la thèse de Dal Co, selon laquelle on peut reconnaître dans les formes de Scarpa des références aux archétypes, que notre culture a oubliés, mais qui sont pourtant encore valables. L'exemplification métaphorique non littérale de ces référents signifierait que l'on tient ces éléments créateurs pour des éléments expressifs. Le passage de l'exemplification à l'expression, qui caractérise le système symbolique de Scarpa, confirmerait sa référence non dénotative et expliquerait la tension poétique dont vivent ses formes architectoniques. Cela permettrait également de comprendre son influence en tant que professeur, au moment où quelques interdits du fonctionnalisme ont perdu de leur importance. Le caractère éminemment pratique des formes fonctionnalistes explique la confusion entre texte et instrument – la maison comme «machine à habiter» –, en raison de laquelle les prétendus formalismes ont été adjugés au domaine de la décoration. En 1963, Carlo Scarpa fut finalement nommé professeur titulaire, toutefois dans la discipline «Decorazione». Quand on songe au peu d'importance qu'avait alors l'ornement, on voit clairement ce que l'Establishment académique de l'époque pensait des recherches de Scarpa dans le domaine de la création architectonique, tout en affirmant le soutenir.

EXPERIENCE DE L'OBJET D'ART

Dans l'architecture de Scarpa, la lumière – pour en venir à un important aspect de sa conception de l'espace – devient le «langage», qui lui permet de placer dans un discours une institution comme le musée et les chefs-d'œuvre qui le constituent, c'est-à-dire les rendre comme formes architectoniques et ainsi les comprendre. Au musée de Possagno par exemple, Scarpa «met au jour» les sculptures de Canova; cette lumière diaphane particulière devient un extraordinaire instrument de la critique architectonique qui fait beaucoup plus d'effet que la version linguistique de la critique d'art. J'avais déjà vu les statues de Canova dans le musée réalisé par Guiseppe Segusini dans les années cin-

La Galleria della Sicilia, Palazzo Abatellis, Palermo
1953–1954; supports for sculptures

From left to right: Bust of Eleonora d'Aragona, head
of a woman, both by Francesco Laurana, head of
a page, attributed to Antonello Gagini

develop to the full the referential complexity of his style. Gottfried Semper's nodes and seams, which, along with facing and texture he declared to be fundamental to architecture, constitute the motifs which permit the static approach to representation to be overcome by pointing towards a programmatic and dynamic dimension. If dancing is the poetic mode of walking, then it is the skill of the carpenter, the stonemason or the weaver which gives form to architectural motifs, translating them into poetic modes of building. If one regards this dynamic, operational concept of figurative representation as a materialist approach to architectural theory, the logical consequence is the abolition of the referential symbolic dimension. When, in the 1960s, I wrote a lecture for my students in which I explained how with Scarpa, a design came about through the drawing process, I described this process as poetic.[3] This aspect provides further motivation for the non-denotative character of Scarpa's compositional language. The language of poetry is centred on itself: it is »opaque« with respect to its content. On this point, Konrad Fiedler's intuitions on the non-transparency of the visual arts are entirely correct, but only by virtue of their specifically poetic-artistic character, and not of their visual nature, as the psychology of visual perception would have it.[4]

In poetic language form is so important that it is difficult if not impossible to distinguish it from the content to which it refers. Seen thus, Scarpa's compositions seem to have no content other than their form. The exemplificatory referentiality and the poetic character of their communication conceal their textual dimension. Scarpa's hinges and joints between his double columns are examples of the clever technology of the scientific apparatus the cut-outs in the panels and the zig-zag outlines are examples of the carpentry of classical architecture. They do not visually reproduce those mechanical technologies found in some engineering transpositions, nor do they reflect the outlines of the orders as in the historicist style. Scarpa's works exemplify the rhythms, the movements and the textures of the referents, in the sense that they share precisely these qualities with them and make their relevance clear. Scarpa's aim was a tighter and more articulated language of formal elements in order to reveal them as shapes.

More recent studies on Scarpa by Francesco Dal Co on the occasion of the 1984 Venice Exhibition attempt to demonstrate a new referentiality in the abstract shapes of his architecture.[5] The conclusions of these studies have been confirmed by the many marginal notes in books offered for inspection by Scarpa's widow, Signora Nini. Scarpa had clearly made repeated use of these works. I agree with Dal Co's thesis that one can

tisch als materialistischen Ansatz, so bedeutet das auch die Aufhebung der referentiellen, symbolischen Dimension.

Als ich in den sechziger Jahren für die Studenten ein Vorlesungsskript vorbereitete, in dem ich darlegte, wie bei Scarpa ein Entwurf vermittels der Zeichnung entstand, bezeichnete ich das als poetisch.[3] Dieser Aspekt ist eine weitere Begründung für den nicht-denotativen Charakter der kompositorischen Referentialität von Scarpas Architektursprache. Die Sprache der Dichtung

quante. Les revoir dans l'annexe de Scarpa fut une véritable révélation. Scarpa a fait de la place aux sculptures en les disposant dans la lumière adéquate: elles constituent elles-mêmes l'espace dans lequel elles se trouvent, si bien qu'il devient impossible de les déplacer ou de les éloigner. Faire de la place dans la lumière, qui est synonyme d'amener à la lumière – créer un espace à l'opposé de l'espace abstrait de la technique moderne[6] –, montre les œuvres d'art et révèle en même temps leur importance. Cette architecture fait com-

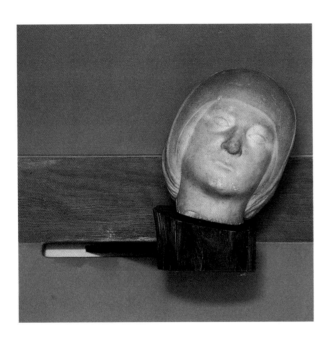

ist nämlich auf sich selbst gerichtet, sie ist »opak« hinsichtlich ihres Inhalts – hier sind Konrad Fiedlers intuitive Überlegungen zur Nichttransparenz der bildenden Kunst durchaus richtig –, aber nur ihres spezifisch künstlerisch-poetischen Charakters wegen, nicht aufgrund ihrer Bildlichkeit wie in der Wahrnehmungspsychologie.[4] In der dichterischen Sprache ist die Form so wichtig, daß ihre Unterscheidung vom Inhalt, auf den sie verweist, schwierig, wenn nicht gar unmöglich wird. So gesehen scheinen die Arbeiten Scarpas keinen anderen Inhalt zu haben als ihre Form. Die exemplifikatorische Referentialität und der poetische Charakter ihrer Kommunikation verbergen deren textuelle Dimension. Scarpas Scharniere und Verbindungen zwischen Doppelsäulen etwa exemplifizieren die raffinierte Technologie der naturwissenschaftlichen Apparaturen, die Schnitte in den Paneelen und die Zackenprofile exemplifizieren Spiegel und Gebälk der klassischen Architektur. Sie geben diese mechanischen Technologien nicht bildlich wieder, wie das bei manchen technizistischen Übertragungen geschieht, und auch nicht die Profile der architektonischen Gliederung wie im historistischen Stil. Die Arbeiten Scarpas exemplifizieren die Rhythmen, die Bewegungsabläufe, die Texturen der Referenten, in dem Sinne, daß sie eben

prendre la thèse de la philosophie de l'art, selon laquelle le travail de celui qui crée l'œuvre d'art et le travail de celui qui la conserve se rencontrent dans la réalisation de l'œuvre d'art. C'est l'œuvre d'art elle-même qui rend possibles ceux qui la réalisent et exige ceux qui la conservent.[7] Selon cette conception, Canova et Scarpa participent tous deux sensiblement à l'état d'œuvre d'art des sculptures à Possagno.

Ainsi, je conçois l'architecture comme un art de la lumière et l'espace comme un instrument de connaissance qui sert à comprendre et à faire comprendre. L'objet du travail d'étude approfondi de Scarpa était donc plutôt les sculptures de Canova que le bâtiment qui devait les abriter. Ce travail est à mon avis très proche de la méthode cultivée par la notion de critique du romantisme: une méthode qui vise la perfection de l'œuvre d'art et non le jugement que l'on porte sur elle. Chez Scarpa, la critique est une expérience de l'œuvre d'art, au cours de laquelle est suscitée la réflexion, à travers laquelle l'œuvre prend conscience d'elle-même.[8] L'architecture de Scarpa fonctionne comme un «système de symboles», comme un langage architectonique qui, parce qu'il est «langage», devient plutôt un «moyen» pour identifier/créer une réalité que l'objet lui-même de l'identification/création.[9] Il me semble es-

detect in Scarpa's formal elements references to archetypal symbols which our civilization has forgotten but which are still active. The non-literal, metaphorical exemplification of these referents entails an Expressionist interpretation of these compositional elements. The alternation between exemplification and expression, the hallmark of Scarpa's symbolic system, would confirm its non-denotative referentiality and explain the poetic tension, two elements which breathe life into his architectual works. It would also explain his influence as a teacher, once certain Functionalist prohibitions had lost their authority. The eminently practical nature of Functionalist forms reflects a confusion between text and tool (the house as a »machine à habiter«), which had relegated Scarpa's so-called formalism to the realm of decoration.

In 1963, Carlo Scarpa was finally made a full professor, but the chair was that of »Decorazione«. Considering the status of »decoration« at that time, we can see what the academic establishment, his self-styled supporters, really thought of his explorations in architectural composition.

EXPERIMENT ON THE WORK OF ART

Light, a very characteristic feature of his designs, in Scarpa's work evolved into the language which enabled him to put into discourse (i. e. put into architectural form), and thus understand, an institution such as a museum along with the works of art which it contained, or rather which constituted it. At the Gipsoteca in Possagno, for example, Scarpa »put into light« on the sculpture of Antonio Canova; it is an especially diaphanous light, which has become an extraordinary instrument of architectural ciriticism, much more effective than the verbiage of the art critics. I had seen the Canova statues once before, in the fifties, before they were moved to Scarpa's annex; to see them here came as a revelation. The architect had put them in just the right light. They are, so to speak, part of the space in which they stand, so that it would be unthinkable to re-arrange or remove them. Placing them in the light like this was an act of enlightenment indeed; in a space contrasting with the abstract space of technical modernity,[6] the works are displayed while their meaning is revealed. This architecture makes comprehensible that thesis of the philosophy of art which maintains that in the creation of a work of art, the labours of those who produce and those who conserve coincide. It is the works themselves which bring their producers into being and require the existence of those who conserve them.[7] Hence, by this interpretation, Antonio Canova and Carlo Scarpa are co-essential to the existence of the sculptures displayed in the Gipsoteca. I should therefore like to consider architecture as the art of light, and

diese Eigenschaften mit ihnen teilen und ihre Relevanz deutlich machen. Scarpas Suche richtete sich auf eine artikuliertere und dichtere Formensprache, um am Ende zu entdecken, daß es eine Sprache der Figuren war.

In neueren Arbeiten zu Scarpa, wie der von Francesco Dal Co anläßlich der Ausstellung von 1984 in Venedig, wird versucht, in den abstrakten Figuren der Architektur Scarpas eine neue, eigene Form der Referentialität nachzuweisen.[5] Bestätigt werden die Ergebnisse dieser Arbeiten durch die vielen Randbemerkungen, die sich in den Büchern finden, die von Signora Nini, der Witwe Scarpas, zur Einsicht bereitgestellt wurden und die Scarpa offensichtlich wiederholt konsultiert hatte. Ich stimme der These von Dal Co durchaus zu, daß man in Scarpas Formen Verweise· auf archetypische Symbole erkennen kann, die unsere Kultur zwar vergessen hat, die aber gleichwohl noch wirksam sind. Die nichtwörtliche, metaphorische Exemplifikation dieser Referenten würde bedeuten, diese Gestaltungselemente für Ausdruckselemente zu halten. Der Wechsel zwischen Exemplifikation und Ausdruck, der das symbolische System Scarpas kennzeichnet, würde seine nicht-denotative Referentialität bestätigen und die poetische Spannung erklären, von der seine architektonischen Formen leben. Das würde auch seinen Einfluß als Lehrer verständlich machen, in dem Augenblick, wo einige Verbote des Funktionalismus an Geltung verloren. Der eminent praktische Charakter der funktionalistischen Formen erklärt die Verwechslung von Text und Werkzeug – das Haus als »machine à habiter« –, aufgrund derer die sogenannten Formalismen von Scarpa dem Bereich der Dekoration zugeschlagen wurden.

1963 wurde Carlo Scarpa schließlich zum ordentlichen Professor berufen, jedoch im Fach »Decorazione«. Wenn man bedenkt, welch geringen Stellenwert damals das Ornament hatte, dann wird deutlich, was das damalige akademische Establishment, das gleichwohl behauptete, ihn zu unterstützen, von Scarpas Erkundungen auf dem Gebiet der architektonischen Gestaltung hielt.

EXPERIMENT AM KUNSTWERK

In Scarpas Architektur wird das Licht – um auf einen wichtigen Aspekt seiner Raumkonzeption zu kommen – zu jener »Sprache«, die es ihm erlaubt, eine Institution wie das Museum und die Kunstwerke, die es konstituieren, in einen Diskurs zu bringen, das heißt, sie in architektonische Formen zu übersetzen und sie damit zu verstehen. Im Museum von Possagno etwa »setzt« Scarpa die Skulpturen von Antonio Canova »ins Licht«; jenes besondere diaphane Licht wird zu einem einzigartigen Instrument der architektonischen Kritik, die sehr

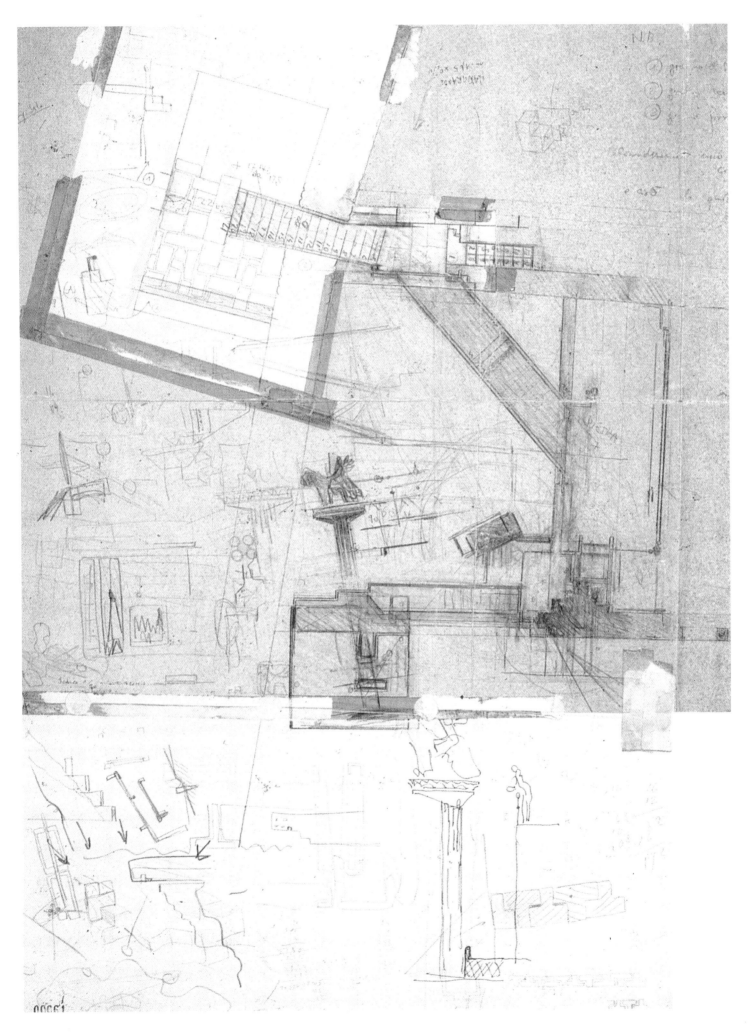

Correr Museum, Venice, 1953; support for
a sculpture

the luminous space created by Scarpa as the cognitive instrument employed to make things clear. Scarpa's explorations were concerned more with Canova's sculptures than with the building which was to house them. The work which Scarpa expended on the Canova statues was architecture used as a form of criticism, but in my opinion a criticism closely akin to the Romantic concept, which viewed criticism as the consummation of a work of art, rather than as a judgement passed on it. For Scarpa, criticism was an experiment on the work of art, awakening the reflection by which the work becomes aware of itself.[8] Scarpa's architecture functions as a system of symbols, as an architectural language, which, being a language, becomes a »means« for the recognition/production of reality rather than the »object« of such a recognition/production.[9] It seems important to me to bring out this reversal of architectural design vis-à-vis Functionalist ideology, according to which – by contrast – the work is what is set up by the search as the goal of understanding.

The hermeneutic approach of Scarpa's architecture explains its critical power and is the key to understanding his zeal to use architecture for the display of works of art, a zeal which characterizes much of his output.

Many of the difficulties experienced by critics in accepting as genuine architecture the work of the occupant of the Chair of »Decorazione« were due to his tendency to design in fragments, to the way in which his projects grew around a pre-existing nucleus, and to his continual revision of what was already on the drawing-board. However, when architecture loses its absolute design character – which also distinguishes the most recent rationalist architectural practice – it becomes an interpretive activity in which, I believe, Scarpa's teaching is of central importance.

Scarpa's work was aimed at local complexities which were becoming increasingly autonomous and independent of any centre or hierarchy. Scarpa did not respond to this loss of a centre with any analytical approach, resolving the whole into ready-made self-sufficient units; rather, he put forward a programme which proceeded piece by piece, the fragmentary nature of which kept open the hermeneutic circularity which characterized the interpretation of texts as well as being the hallmark of Scarpa's architecture.

To this insight that things belong together, an insight which brings to a focus the relational character of Scarpa's details, can be added another aspect of the relationship between the whole and its parts, namely an awareness of the dialogue in which the design came about. Scarpa's work always implies an interplay between those who speak the same language, who share a particular system of symbols. The design process, if understood as interpretive, is based on the understand-

Previous page: Castelvecchio Museum, Verona
1956–1964; drawing of Cangrande space

viel wirkungsvoller ist als die sprachliche Version der Kunstkritik.

Ich hatte die Canova-Statuen schon in den fünfziger Jahren in dem von Giuseppe Segusini gestalteten Museum gesehen. Sie nun im Erweiterungsbau von Scarpa wiederzusehen war eine regelrechte Offenbarung. Scarpa schaffte den Skulpturen Platz, indem er sie ins richtige Licht setzte: Sie selbst konstituieren den Raum, in dem sie stehen, so daß es geradezu undenkbar wird, sie von dort zu verrücken oder zu entfernen. Dieses Platzschaffen im Licht, das ein Ans-Licht-Bringen bedeutet – ein Raumschaffen, das im Gegensatz steht zum abstrakten Raum der modernen Technik[6] –, zeigt die Kunstwerke und enthüllt zugleich ihre Bedeutung. In dieser Architektur wird die These der Kunstphilosophie verständlich, wonach in der Herstellung des Kunstwerks die Arbeit dessen, der es schafft, und dessen, der es bewahrt, zusammentreffen. Das Kunstwerk selbst macht diejenigen möglich, die es herstellen, und verlangt diejenigen, die es bewahren.[7] So sind nach dieser Auffassung Canova und Scarpa gleich wesentlich beteiligt am Kunstwerk-sein der Skulpturen in Possagno.

So verstehe ich die Architektur als eine Kunst des Lichts und den Raum als ein Erkenntnisinstrument, das dem Verstehen und Verständlichmachen dient. Gegenstand der explorativen Entwurfsarbeit von Scarpa waren also eher die Skulpturen von Canova als das Gebäude, das sie beherbergen sollte. Diese Arbeit ist meines Erachtens jener Methode sehr verwandt, die der Kritikbegriff der Romantik entwickelt hat: eine Methode, die auf die Vollendung des Kunstwerks abzielt statt auf seine Beurteilung. Bei Scarpa ist die Kritik ein Experiment am Kunstwerk, bei dem Reflexion wachgerufen wird, durch die das Werk zum Bewußtsein seiner selbst gebracht wird.[8] Scarpas Architektur funktioniert wie ein »Symbolsystem«, wie eine Architektursprache, die, weil sie »Sprache« ist, eher zum »Mittel« für das Erkennen/Herstellen einer Realität wird, als der Gegenstand selbst der Erkenntnis/Herstellung zu sein.[9] Mir scheint es wichtig, diese Umkehrung des architektonischen Entwurfs hinsichtlich der Ideologie des Funktionalismus hervorzuheben, bei der im Gegensatz dazu das Werk das ist, was die Suche als Erkenntnisziel setzt. Der hermeneutische Ansatz der Architektur Scarpas erklärt ihre kritische Kraft und macht auch das Engagement verständlich, mit dem Scarpa die Architektur für die Präsentation von Kunstwerken – einem Schwerpunkt seines gesamten Schaffens – einsetzte.

Manche der Schwierigkeiten der Kritik, das Werk Scarpas, des ordentlichen Professors für »Decorazione«, als Architektur zu akzeptieren, rührt von seiner Art her, in Fragmenten zu entwerfen, von der Art, wie seine Konstruktionen sich um einen schon vorhandenen Nukleus

sentiel de souligner ce renversement du projet architectonique quant à l'idéologie du fonctionnalisme où, au contraire, l'œuvre est ce que la recherche se fixe comme objectif de l'identification. Le début herméneutique de l'architecture de Scarpa explique son pouvoir critique et permet également de comprendre l'engagement avec lequel Scarpa utilisait l'architecture pour présenter des œuvres d'art – le point capital de toute sa création.

Certaines difficultés qu'eut la critique pour accepter comme architecture l'œuvre de Scarpa, professeur titulaire de «Decorazione», sont dues à sa manière de concevoir par fragments, à la manière dont ses constructions se développent autour d'un noyau déjà existant, aux retouches permanentes qu'il faisait à ses dessins. Quand l'architecture renonce toutefois à l'idée du caractère absolu du dessin, qui est également caractéristique de la pratique architecturale rationaliste récente, elle finit par devenir une activité herméneutique, et les idées de Scarpa ont, à mon avis, une importance capitale pour comprendre.

Le travail de conception de Scarpa se concentrait avant tout sur des complexités locales qui devenaient de plus en plus autonomes et de plus en plus indépendantes d'un centre ou d'une hiérarchie quelconques. L'architecture de Scarpa n'a pas répondu à cette perte de centre par un début d'analyse en décomposant le tout en unités complètes et autarciques, mais en présentant une sorte de projection qui agissait petit à petit. La partialité de ces fragments laisse ouvert le cercle herméneutique qui caractérise l'interprétation de textes et l'œuvre architectonique de Scarpa. Cette compréhension pour ce qui est compatible, qui voit le caractère relationnel des détails chez Scarpa, peut, à mon avis, être en outre liée à un autre aspect de ce rapport entre le tout et ses parties: la conscience de la situation dialoguée dans laquelle le dessin est placé. L'œuvre de Scarpa implique toujours un entretien entre les membres d'une communauté linguistique, qui partagent un système de symboles précis. Le travail de l'ébauche, si on le conçoit comme travail herméneutique, se base sur cette compréhension de l'appartenance de l'œuvre à un contexte précis et sur l'emploi d'un langage architectonique spécifique.[10] Cette caractérisation du travail de l'ébauche de Scarpa aboutit à la question du rôle de la restauration et de l'histoire.

PROJET ET HISTOIRE

Quand Scarpa développait de nouveaux projets dans des contextes historiques, cette prédilection consistant à construire dans le construit était considérée comme un défaut, si bien que Bruno Zevi – qui soutenait absolument le résultat – se vit contraint de dire que Scarpa était «un grand artiste, mais pas un architecte». Aujour-

Setting for the monument to the Women of the
Resistance by A. Murer, Venice, 1968

Following picture page: Rearrangement of the
»Aula magna« of Ca'Foscari, Venice,
1955–1956

ing that the project belongs to a particular context using
a particular architectural language.[10] This description
of Scarpa's approach to design leads us to the question
of restoration and history.

DESIGN AND CONTEXT

When Scarpa worked on new projects in historical contexts, this preference of his for building on existing
structures was much deprecated, and even Bruno Zevi,
who was never backward in expressing his support for
the results, felt compelled to describe Scarpa as »a
great artist, but not an architect«. Today, this interest is
looked upon as Scarpa's greatest virtue. Opposing contemporary trends in architecture, he refused to heed the
siren voices of utopianism, and explored regions remote from the missionary zeal of the ideologists. Since
Scarpa, it has come to be recognized that many of the
designs of the great architects of the past were likewise
developed in historical contexts: Brunelleschi, Alberti,
Bramante, Palladio and Borromini all built, like Scarpa,
on the existing structures.

herumentwickeln, seinem ständigen Überarbeiten dessen, was schon in der Zeichnung vorlag. Wenn jedoch die Architektur die Auffassung vom absoluten Charakter des Entwurfs aufgibt, die auch kennzeichnend ist für die jüngste rationalistische Architekturpraxis, dann wird sie endlich zu einer hermeneutischen Tätigkeit, für deren Verständnis die Einsichten Scarpas von zentraler Bedeutung sind.

Scarpas Gestaltungsarbeit richtete sich vor allem auch auf lokale Komplexitäten, die zunehmend autonomer, unabhängiger von irgendeinem Zentrum oder einer Hierarchie wurden. Auf diesen Verlust des Zentrums antwortete Scarpas Architektur nicht mit einem analytischen Ansatz, indem sie das Ganze in abgeschlossene, selbstgenügsame Einheiten zerlegte, sondern indem sie eine Art der Projektierung vorstellt, die stückweise vorging. Die Partialität dieser Fragmente hält jenen hermeneutischen Zirkel offen, der die Interpretation von Texten kennzeichnet und eben auch Scarpas Architekturschaffen charakterisiert. Diese Einsicht in das Zusammengehören, die den relationalen Charakter der Details bei Scarpa im Blick hat, läßt sich meines Erachtens noch mit einem anderen Aspekt dieses Verhältnisses vom Ganzen und seinen Teilen verbinden: das Bewußtsein für die dialogische Situation, in die der Entwurf gestellt ist. Das Werk Scarpas impliziert immer ein Gespräch zwischen den Mitgliedern einer Sprachgemeinschaft, die ein bestimmtes Symbolsystem teilen. Die Arbeit des Entwerfens, versteht man sie als hermeneutische Arbeit, gründet auf dieser Einsicht in die Zugehörigkeit des Werks zu einem bestimmten Kontext und auf der Verwendung einer spezifischen Architektursprache.[10] Diese Kennzeichnung der Entwurfsarbeit Scarpas führt zu der Frage nach der Rolle von Restaurierung und Geschichte.

ENTWURF UND GESCHICHTE

Als Scarpa neue Projekte in historischen Kontexten entwickelte, betrachtete man diese Vorliebe von ihm, im schon Gebauten zu bauen, als Mangel, so daß Bruno Zevi – der das Resultat durchaus unterstützte – sich zu der Äußerung veranlaßt sah, Scarpa sei »ein großer Künstler, aber kein Architekt«. Heute erscheint dieses Interesse Scarpas als sein größtes Verdienst. Seine dem Zeitgeist zuwiderlaufende Architektur, die nicht auf die Sirenen des modernen Utopismus hörte, hatte Bereiche zu erkunden gewußt, die dem missionarischen Lärm der gängigen Planideologien einigermaßen fernlagen. Nach Scarpa erkennt man nun, daß ein Großteil der von den großen Architekten der Vergangenheit entwickelten Entwürfe ebenfalls in historischen Kontexten situiert waren: Brunelleschi, Alberti, Bramante, Palladio oder Borromini hatten wie Scarpa im schon Gebauten gebaut. Scarpas Neigung, Neues in historische Kon-

d'hui, la prédilection de Scarpa semble être son plus grand mérite. Son architecture allant à l'encontre de l'esprit du siècle, qui n'écoutait pas les sirènes de l'utopisme moderne, avait su explorer des domaines en quelque sorte éloignés de l'esprit missionnaire des idéologies habituelles. Après Scarpa, on reconnaît maintenant qu'une grande partie des projets élaborés par les grands architectes du passé étaient également situés dans des contextes historiques: Brunelleschi, Alberti, Bramante, Palladio ou Borromini avaient construit dans le construit comme Scarpa. On peut, à mon avis, établir un rapport entre la tendance de Scarpa à projeter du nouveau dans des contextes historiques et une autre de ses prédilections, à savoir son intérêt pour l'aménagement de musées. Ce qui lie ces deux prédilections, c'est sa capacité de «lecture», compétence qui lui permet de déchiffrer des «textes visuels» tels que le bâtiment existant ou les tableaux et les statues. Nous avons donc lié trois thèmes qui me paraissent essentiels pour comprendre l'architecture de Carlo Scarpa: le projet, qui repose sur la réflexion dite «visuelle», l'intérêt pour l'aménagement de musées et la restauration créative de bâtiments existants. Dans tous ces cas, Scarpa travaillait comme s'il avait une sorte d'entretien architectonique avec les figures de forme rencontrées. Ses musées ne sont jamais des espaces neutres qui seraient ouverts pour l'expositition d'œuvres d'art quelconques, ce sont au contraire des interventions critiques qui – partant des œuvres d'art – représentent des compléments qui achèvent et sont essentiels pour leur compréhension. Le projet insère aussi dans le construit les composantes critiques au travers desquels l'œuvre d'art originale parvient à la conscience de soi-même, il fait de nouveau parler le bâtiment existant en transformant son contexte.

Cette approche de la création architectonique, que j'ai comparée à la création visuelle des artistes-bâtisseurs de la Renaissance, représente donc une réponse à la question relative aux rapports entre l'histoire et le projet. Scarpa emploie un langage visuel dont l'effet est garanti par son historicité intrinsèque. Son rapport avec l'histoire n'a rien à voir avec l'historisme académique qui utilise l'étude et la contemplation de l'architecture du passé pour en tirer des motifs, des formes ou des dispositions comme si c'était un magasin de «phrases toutes faites» – pour reprendre une expression d'Adolf Loos. Pour Scarpa, l'histoire tenait prêt le répertoire établi de la tradition dont se nourrit l'importance des figures que fait naître le dessin du projet. On reconnaît dans ses interventions architectoniques cette communauté de langage, ce «lexique familial» qui relie entre eux les différents arts plastiques dans le dessin. Quand la réalisation d'un projet se prolonge au-delà de la mort d'un architecte, sa finition doit pouvoir être réalisée par

texte zu projizieren, läßt sich, so meine ich, mit seiner anderen Vorliebe in Zusammenhang bringen, nämlich seinem Interesse an der Einrichtung von Museen. Was diese beiden Vorlieben miteinander verbindet, ist seine Fähigkeit zu »lesen«, eben jene Kompetenz, die es ihm erlaubt, »visuelle Texte« wie das schon vorhandene Gebäude oder die Bilder und Statuen zu dechiffrieren. Wir haben also drei Themen miteinander verknüpft, die mir grundlegend zu sein scheinen für das Verständnis der Architektur von Carlo Scarpa: der Entwurf, der auf der genannten »visuellen« Reflexion beruht, das Interesse für die Einrichtung von Museen und die kreative Restaurierung von vorhandenen Gebäuden. In allen diesen Fällen arbeitete Scarpa so, als ob er eine Art architektonisches Gespräch mit den vorgefundenen Formfiguren führt. Seine Museen sind niemals neutrale Räume, die offen wären für die Aufstellung beliebiger Kunstwerke, sie sind vielmehr kritische Eingriffe, die – ausgehend von den Kunstwerken – vollendende Komplementierungen darstellen, die wesentlich für deren Verständnis sind. Auch in das schon Gebaute fügt der Entwurf jene kritischen Komplemente ein, durch die das ursprüngliche Kunstwerk zum Bewußtsein seiner selbst gelangt. Er bringt das schon vorhandene Gebäude wieder zum Sprechen, indem er seinen Kontext umgestaltet.

Diese Herangehensweise an die architektonische Gestaltung, die ich mit der visuellen Gestaltung der Künstler-Baumeister der Renaissance verglichen habe, ist daher auch eine Antwort auf die Frage nach dem Verhältnis von Geschichte und Entwurf. Scarpa verwendet eine visuelle Sprache, deren Wirksamkeit durch ihre intrinsische Historizität gewährleistet ist. Sein Verhältnis zur Geschichte hat nichts mit jenem akademischen Historismus zu tun, der Studium und Anschauung der Architektur der Vergangenheit dazu benutzt, ihr Motive, Formen oder Anordnungen wie einer Vorratskammer von »fertigen Phrasen« – um einen Ausdruck von Adolf Loos zu verwenden – zu entnehmen. Für Scarpa hielt die Geschichte vielmehr den etablierten Bestand der Tradition bereit, aus dem sich die Bedeutung der Figuren, die die Zeichnung des Entwurfs aufruft, speist. Man erkennt bei seinen architektonischen Eingriffen eben diese Gemeinsamkeit der Sprache, dieses »Familienlexikon«, das die verschiedenen bildenden Künste in der Zeichnung miteinander verbindet. Wenn sich die Realisierung eines Projekts über den Tod eines Architekten hinaus hinzieht, dann muß seine Fertigstellung von einem Interpreten geleistet werden können, der die Sprache kennt und daher in der Lage ist, das Bauwerk auch zu vollenden. Dieses Vervollständigen des Entwurfs, der von einer Generation zur nächsten weitergetragen wird – was bei der Errichtung von Gebäuden recht häufig geschieht –, wird zum Normalfall

un interprète qui connaît le langage et est en mesure d'achever le bâtiment. Ce parachèvement du projet, qui est poursuivi d'une génération à l'autre – ce qui arrive très souvent dans la construction de bâtiments –, devient la norme dans la formation de l'architecture publique. Les places et les rues constituent des espaces dont les murs sont formés par les façades de maisons construites au cours de diverses époques. La continuité du projet devient alors une affaire pour ainsi dire précaire quand cette communauté de langage fait défaut. Le système visuel de l'architecture de Carlo Scarpa représente donc une contribution originale pour ce qui est de surmonter les nombreuses difficultés que rencontre le projet actuel quand il intervient dans des contextes historiques.

LUMIERE ET ESPACE

Quand Scarpa adopta son langage architectonique, son intention était de transformer l'acte de la construction en opération de la connaissance et de la communication. Konrad Fiedler avait expliqué cet aspect de la connaissance de l'action artistique dans un essai consacré à l'architecture et avait pris les théories de Gottfried Semper pour point de départ de ses propres réflexions théoriques.[11] Pour mieux comprendre cet aspect de la théorie de la connaissance contenu dans la projection, nous allons examiner la transformation du langage créateur de Scarpa en langage de la Sécession et fixer cette transformation à un élément structurel décisif pour les nouvelles voies de l'architecture moderne, à savoir la fenêtre.[12]

Ce n'est pas un hasard si la fenêtre assume un rôle remarquable dans l'interprétation de l'architecture pour ce qui est du contexte et des particularités régionales. Si l'on fixe son attention sur la fenêtre, on peut alors observer comment les ouvertures des façades conçues comme «chapelles», «loggias» ou «porches», se transforment en ouvertures prévues comme «bay windows». Au cours d'une autre phase d'évolution, qui conduisit Scarpa au nouveau sens de l'espace, les ouvertures conçues comme «bay windows» se transforment en fenêtres d'angle. Cette deuxième phase – encore plus décisive que la première – est en même temps l'étape allant de la Sécession au Néo-plasticisme, tel que l'incarnait Frank Lloyd Wright. Comme Scarpa, Neutra et Schindler ont également repris cette découverte, tout en conservant le sens des constructions artisanalement solides. Je ne veux naturellement pas dire que l'architecture de Scarpa doit être comparée à celle de Schindler et de Neutra, il me semble toutefois intéressant de comprendre ce nouveau sens de l'espace qui avait déjà influencé Mies van der Rohe et avant lui les Hollandais, qui devaient par la suite développer l'architecture du mouvement De Stijl.[13]

35

Carlo Scarpa with Arrigo Rudi, discussing the building of the Banca Popolare di Verona

Scarpa's preference for designing new things in a historical context should be seen alongside his other favourite activity, museum design. The link between these two predilections was his ability to »read«, to decipher »visual texts«, in the form of an existing building or in the pictures and sculptures which were to be displayed. It is this peculiar faculty, this visual competence, which characterizes Scarpa's creative process. Thus we have drawn together three threads which seem to me fundamental to an understanding of his architecture: his design process, based on this visual competence, his interest in museum design, and his creative restoration of existing buildings. In all these instances, Scarpa seemed to develop an architectural dialogue with the existing shapes. His museums are never merely neutral spaces into which any old works of art could be inserted; rather, they represent critical and conscious decisions, which, taking the exhibits as their starting point, complement them in a way essential to their understanding, they are – as a new museology suggests – installations. This approach to architectural composition, which I have compared to the visual approach of the Renaissance painter-architects, also provides an answer to the relation between project and history. Scarpa employed a visual language whose effectiveness was backed up by an intrinsic historicity. His attitude to history has nothing in common with the sort of academic historicism which uses a study of the architecture of the past to exploit its themes, shapes and lay-outs as though it were a warehouse of »ready-made phrases«, to use an expression of Adolf Loos'. For Scarpa, history was a codex consolidated by tradition, breathing meaning into the shapes conjured up on the design by drawing. On can discern his architectural approach this common language, this familar vocabulary, which links the different visual arts across the whole design. If a project continues after the death of its architect, it must be finished by someone who, knowing this language, can bring it to completion. This handing-down of a project from generation to generation, common enough anyway, is now becoming the norm where »civic architecture« is concerned. Squares and streets are »rooms«, whose interior walls are the façades of houses dating from different epochs. Continuity would be precarious if there were no shared language. Scarpa's visual system in architecture is thus an original contribution towards overcoming the many difficulties facing contemporary designers when they enter a historical context.

LIGHT AND SPACE

Having adopted a system of architecture akin to that of the Secession, Scarpa wanted to turn the act of construction into a process of communication and under-

bei der Herausbildung der öffentlichen Architektur. Plätze und Straßen schaffen Räume, deren Wände durch die Fassaden der Häuser gebildet werden, die in verschiedenen Epochen entstanden sind. Dort wird die Kontinuität des Projektentwurfs zu einer einigermaßen prekären Angelegenheit, wenn eben jene Gemeinsamkeit in der Sprache fehlt. Das visuelle System der Architektur Scarpas stellt deshalb einen originellen Beitrag zur Überwindung der vielen Schwierigkeiten dar, die der Entwurf der Gegenwart antrifft, wenn er einen Eingriff in historische Kontexte unternimmt.

LICHT UND RAUM

Als Scarpa sich eine Architektursprache zu eigen machte, war es seine Absicht, auch den Akt des Bauens zu einem Prozeß der Erkenntnis und der Kommunikation zu machen. Diesen Erkenntnisaspekt des künstlerischen Tuns hatte Konrad Fiedler in einem der Architektur gewidmeten Aufsatz erläutert, in dem er die Theorien von Gottfried Semper zum Ausgangspunkt seiner eigenen theoretischen Überlegungen genommen hatte.[11] Um diesen in der Projektierung enthaltenen erkenntnistheoretischen Aspekt besser zu verstehen, wollen wir uns die Entwicklung von Scarpas Gestaltungssprache zu derjenigen der Sezession anschauen und diese Entwicklung an einem für die neuen Wege der modernen Architektur entscheidenden Kompositionselement, nämlich dem Fenster, festmachen.[12]

Das Fenster übernimmt nicht zufällig eine hervorragende Rolle bei der Interpretation der Architektur im Hinblick auf Kontextbedingungen und regionale Eigenheiten. Richtet man seine Aufmerksamkeit auf das Fenster, so kann man die Entwicklung verfolgen, wie aus den Öffnungen der Fassaden, intendiert als »Ädikula«, als »Loggia« oder als »Vorhalle«, Öffnungen werden, die als »bay windows« vorgesehen sind. In einem weiteren Entwicklungsschritt, der Scarpa an das neue Raumempfinden heranführte, werden die als »bay windows« intendierten Öffnungen zu Eckfenstern. Dieser zweite Schritt – noch entscheidender als der erste – ist zugleich der Schritt von der Sezession zum Neoplastizismus, wie ihn Frank Lloyd Wright verkörperte. Wie Scarpa griffen auch Neutra und Schindler diese Entdeckung auf, bewahrten sich dabei aber den Sinn für handwerklich solide Konstruktionen. Ich meine natürlich nicht, daß Scarpa in seiner Architektur mit Schindler und Neutra zu vergleichen sei, mir scheint es jedoch interessant, dieses neue Raumempfinden zu begreifen, das schon Mies beeinflußt hatte und vor ihm schon jene Niederländer, die dann die Architektur des De Stijl entwickeln sollten.[13] Diese neue Raumkonzeption wurde von Wright sehr prägnant in einer immer wiederkehrenden Begründung beschrieben: die Zerstörung der Schachtel.[14] Scarpa übernahm diesen Raum, den er

Cette nouvelle conception de l'espace fut décrite de manière frappante par Wright dans une justification périodique: la destruction de la boîte.[14] Scarpa reprit cet espace qu'il obtint en défaisant les coins traditionnels, mais en garnissant les surfaces ainsi dissociées de charnières. On a montré à juste titre que le mouvement De Stijl représente la codification systématique du langage architectonique moderne; si l'on accepte aussi les surfaces courbes et les dispositions non rectangulaires, le système néo-plastique et le programme en cinq points de Le Corbusier représentent ensemble la déformation la plus répandue de la grammaire architectonique.[15]

Je veux maintenant reprendre et examiner de plus près le paradigme de l'espace comme «abat-jour renversé», c'est-à-dire comment on parvient de l'espace composé du système architectonique classique à l'espace composé de l'architecture de la Sécession afin de pouvoir décrire ensuite le passage au langage architectonique du mouvement De Stijl. Pour comprendre l'importance de ces observations, il faut rappeler les paramètres de la construction/description de l'espace éclairé: les sources lumineuses et les diffuseurs de lumière. Les pièces pourvues de fenêtres sont des combinaisons spécifiques de sources lumineuses et de diffuseurs de lumière. Nous avons d'une part les espaces presque entièrement en verre de l'architecture gothique, d'autre part les espaces de l'architecture classique avec leurs ouvertures régulières fournies par les chapelles et les porches. De même, il y a d'un côté les espaces des pays nordiques, qui sont pourvus de «bay windows» afin de pouvoir mieux capter la lumière grâce à de grandes «surfaces de réception», de l'autre les espaces protégés des pays méridionaux qui doivent se protéger contre la lumière. En tant qu'invention des temps modernes, la fenêtre d'angle a pour conséquence un espace dans lequel les sources lumineuses – les ouvertures en verre – et les diffuseurs de lumière – les murs qui la reflètent – se rencontrent perpendiculairement. Cette solution évite l'effet de contre-jour que font naître les fenêtres quand elles se trouvent au milieu du mur, où seuls les domaines éloignés de la source peuvent faire office de diffuseurs de lumière. Si l'on comprend que l'on peut modeler la lumière en disposant les surfaces lumineuses et les diffuseurs de lumière de manière appropriée, on peut également obtenir une nouvelle qualité de création architectonique. Dans ses bâtiments, Scarpa utilisait les surfaces colorées, les murs blancs ou l'eau comme diffuseurs de lumière et les combinait avec différentes sources lumineuses directes, indirectes ou artificielles. Comme Scarpa ordonnait les sources lumineuses et les surfaces distributrices de lumière perpendiculairement les unes par rapport aux autres, comme c'est le cas pour les fenêtres d'angle, les murs se transformaient en systèmes d'illu-

standing. This »understanding« aspect of the artistic process has been explained by Conrad Fiedler in an essay devoted to architecture, in which he based his own reflections on the theories of Gottfried Semper.[11] In order to reach a better understanding of this aspect of design, we should look at the transition of Scarpa's compositional system towards that of the Secession, by reference to one decisive element of composition in modern architecture, namely the window.[12]

It is no coincidence that windows play an important role in the interpretation of architecture from the point of view of immediate surroundings and regional context. A study of the window makes it possible to trace its development from an opening in the frontage intended as an »aedicula«, or »loggia« or »porch«, to an opening intended as a »bay-window«. A further development, leading Scarpa to a new concept of space, made possible the step from »bay-windows« to »corner windows«.

This second step, even more decisive than the first, was the transition from Secession to Neo-Plasticism, embodied in the work of Frank Lloyd Wright. Neutra and Schindler, like Scarpa, took up this discovery, while preserving their feeling for solid craftsmanship. I do not, of course, mean to compare Scarpa's architecture to that of Schindler and Neutra, but it is interesting to recognize this new concept of space, which had influenced Mies van der Rohe and before him the Dutchmen who developed the architecture of De Stijl.[13] The new concept was described most succinctly by Wright in »The Destruction of the Box«.[14] Scarpa adopted it, eliminating the traditional corners of rooms, but provided the dissociated surfaces with highly articulated joints. It has been pointed out, and rightly, that De Stijl represents the most systematic codification of modern architectural language; if one accepts curved surfaces and non-orthogonal lay-outs, Neo-Plasticism, along with Le Corbusier's »5-point system« is the most widespread version of modern architectural »grammar«.[15] I shall take the metaphor of the room intended as an inverted lampshade, and consider more closely how the change came about from rooms in the classical style to those built under the Secession, in order to describe the transition to De Stijl. To understand the relevance of these observations we must bear in mind the chief variables in an illuminated space, light sources and light diffusers. Rooms with windows – inverted lampshades, we have called them – are particular combinations of light sources and light diffusers. On the one hand, we have the almost completely glazed rooms of Gothic architecture; on the other, we have Classical architecture with its regular apertures and niches and porches. In the northern countries, rooms have bay-windows to catch as much light as possible,

dadurch erreichte, daß er die traditionellen Ecken auflöste, aber die so dissoziierten Flächen mit sehr artikulierten Verbindungen versah. Es ist mit Recht gezeigt worden, daß der De Stijl die systematische Kodifizierung der modernen Architektursprache darstellt; akzeptiert man auch gekrümmte Flächen und nicht-rechtwinklige Anordnungen, dann stellt das neoplastische System zusammen mit dem 5-Punkte-Programm von Le Corbusier die verbreitetste Ausformung der modernen Architekturgrammatik dar.[15]

Ich will hier das Paradigma vom Raum als »umgekehrtem Lampenschirm« aufgreifen und näher betrachten, wie man vom zusammengesetzten Raum im klassischen Architektursystem zu der Art von Zusammensetzung des Raums in der Architektur der Sezession gelangte, um dann den Übergang von dort zur Architektursprache des De Stijl beschreiben zu können. Um die Relevanz dieser Beobachtungen zu verstehen, muß man an die Parameter für die Konstruktion/Deskription des ausgeleuchteten Raums erinnern: Lichtquellen und Lichtverteiler. Räume mit Fenstern sind spezifische Kombinationen von Lichtquellen und Lichtverteilern. Auf der einen Seite haben wir die nahezu vollständig gläsernen Räume der gotischen Architektur, auf der anderen Seite die Räume der klassischen Architektur mit ihren regelmäßigen Öffnungen, vermittelt durch Nischen und Vorhallen. Und ebenso gibt es auf der einen Seite die Räume der nördlichen Länder, die mit »bay windows« versehen sind, um mit großen »Auffangflächen« das wenige Licht besser sammeln zu können, auf der anderen Seite die abgeschirmten Räume der südlichen Länder, die sich gegen zuviel Licht schützen müssen.

Das Eckfenster als Erfindung der Moderne bewirkt einen Raum, in dem die Lichtquellen – die Glasöffnungen – und die Lichtverteiler – die Wände, die es reflektieren – senkrecht aufeinandertreffen. Diese Lösung vermeidet jenen Gegenlichteffekt, den die Fenster hervorrufen, wenn sie in der Mitte der Wand angebracht sind, wo nur die von der Quelle entfernten Bereiche als Lichtverteiler fungieren können. Wenn man begreift, daß man das Licht dadurch gestalten kann, daß man Lichtquellen und Lichtverteiler entsprechend zweckmäßig anordnet, kann man auch eine neue architektonische Gestaltungsqualität erreichen. Scarpa benutzte bei seinen Gebäuden als Lichtverteiler farbige Oberflächen, weiße Wände oder Wasser etc. und kombinierte sie mit verschiedenen Lichtquellen, seien sie direkter, indirekter oder künstlicher Art. Indem er Lichtquelle und lichtverteilende Fläche rechtwinklig zueinander anordnete, wie das bei den Eckfenstern geschieht, wurden die Wände zu illuminierenden Systemen, die das Licht mit ihrer Materialstruktur färben. So werden jene Techniken verständlich und damit wiederholbar, mit

Previous page: Gipsoteca Canoviana, Possagno, 1955–1957; corner window in the extension

Following picture page: Banca Popolare di Verona, Verona, 1973–1981; solutions for windows in the main façade

Carlo Scarpa with Arrigo Rudi and Domenico Sandri during building work at the Banca Popolare di Verona

while rooms in Mediterranean lands have to be protected from the sunlight by shades and blinds. Corner windows, an invention of the Modernist movement, produce a room in which the glazed apertures – the light sources – and the walls – the surfaces which diffuse this light – are at right angles to each other. This solution avoids the dazzle resulting from a window in the middle of the wall, where the only diffusers are well away from the light source. Once it is realized that light can be modulated by an opportune combination of sources and diffusers, a new level of architectural quality becomes possible.

Scarpa used coloured surfaces, white walls, water etc., as diffusers in his buildings combining them with various sources of direct, indirect or artificial light. With light sources and diffusing surfaces at right angles to each other, as with corner windows, the walls become illumination systems which colour the light through their own material texture.

Furthermore, one compositional technique introduced by Scarpa may, I think, be derived from the architecture of the towns in the Veneto. For this purpose, it is sufficient to recall Scarpa's projects of the 1950s, with their corner-windows. Apart from the Possagno gallery, these include the Casa Veritti in Udine, and some unfinished projects such as the Casa Zoppas in Conegliano and the Casa Taddei in Venice. He translated the corner-windows of the new spatial concept into the vocabulary of the Veneto.

The light produced by these corner-windows becomes a chromatic luminosity full of transparency, typical of the region's visual arts for centuries. In the Venezuelan pavilion on the Venice Biennale site, Scarpa covered the corner windows between the two halls with latticed shades, reminiscent of similar solutions to the problem of filtering the light. His rooms have a luminosity which, apart from the manifestly different vocabulary, generate the flowing light of Palladio and his 17th and 18th century successors.

Along the way, Scarpa's Venetian language was enriched by other important design elements when he moved from shaded corner-windows to the double façade claddings borrowed by Louis Kahn and Robert Venturi, I believe from the Baroque.[16] For the Banca Popolare di Verona he designed windows of the type he had seen many years before in an ugly building in Genoa while staying in the Hotel Bristol across the street.

Scarpa pointed out to me that the new openings in the external cladding were of different shape, and smaller, than the windows in the inner wall. He realized that the light reflected by the glass would be diffused by the inner surface of the outer cladding, thus reducing glare and improving the lighting within. This solution, even

denen Scarpa den Effekt der diffusen Helligkeit erzeugte, die beispielsweise den Raum des Museums in Possagno auszeichnet.

Des weiteren kann man, so meine ich, das von Scarpa in die Architektur eingeführte Kompositionsverfahren auf die Stadtarchitektur des Veneto zurückführen. Für Beispiele dieser Entwicklungsschritte genügt es, an Scarpas Projekte der fünfziger Jahre zu erinnern, an Gebäude, in denen die Räume offene und verglaste Ecken besitzen. Neben dem Museum in Possagno stellen die Casa Veritti in Udine und einige der nicht realisierten Projekte wie die Casa Zoppas in Conegliano und die Casa Taddei in Venedig gute Beispiele für die Entwicklung der Architektur Scarpas dar. Er übersetzte die Eckfenster der neuen Raumauffassung in die Sprache des Veneto: Das Licht, das diese Eckfenster erzeugen, wird zur chromatischen, aus Transparenzen entstehenden, leuchtenden Helligkeit, die den für die Werke der bildenden Kunst dieser Region seit Jahrhunderten typischen Charakter aufweist. Im Venezuela-Pavillon auf dem Biennale-Gelände in Venedig überzog Scarpa die Eckfenster, die die beiden Ausstellungsräume miteinander verbinden, mit abschattenden Gittern, die an andere, analoge Lösungen zur Filterung des Lichtes erinnern. Seine Räume entstehen aus einer leuchtenden Helligkeit, die, abgesehen von den evidenten Unterschieden im Vokabular, das fließende Licht Palladios und der nachfolgenden Architektur des 17. und 18. Jahrhunderts erzeugt.

Auf diesem Wege wird die dem Veneto verbundene Architektursprache Scarpas durch andere wichtige Gestaltungselemente bereichert, wenn er den Schritt tut von den abgeschatteten Eckfenstern zur doppelten Fassadenverkleidung, die Louis Kahn und Robert Venturi meines Wissens der Barockarchitektur entnahmen.[16]

Für die Banca Popolare di Verona hat Scarpa Fenster entworfen, die er etliche Jahre zuvor vom Zimmer des Bristol Hotels in Genua aus an einem häßlichen Gebäude gegenüber gesehen hatte – als er sich dort im Zusammenhang mit dem geplanten Neubau des Teatro di Genua aufhielt. Die neugeschaffenen Öffnungen in der äußeren Verkleidung dieses Gebäudes hatten, darauf machte mich Scarpa aufmerksam, eine andere Form und waren kleiner als die Fenster in der inneren Wand des Gebäudes. Scarpa wußte, daß auf diese Weise das vom Glas reflektierte Licht von der inneren Fläche der äußeren Verkleidung verteilt würde und damit den Gegenlichteffekt abmildern und die Raumhelligkeit steigern würde. Diese Lösung, die sich der Architektur Palladios und des Veneto – mit den stratifizierten und transparenten Flächen – noch stärker annäherte, erlaubte die Verwendung von Fenstern in der Wandmitte ohne die Folge lästiger Blendungseffekte. Ein solcher Raum, dessen Charakter von der doppelten

mination colorant la lumière grâce à leur structure concrète. Les techniques, grâce auxquelles Scarpa créait l'effet de clarté diffuse qui caractérise par exemple l'espace du musée de Possagno, sont ainsi compréhensibles et peuvent donc être répétées.

Je pense qu'il est en outre possible de ramener le procédé de composition introduit dans l'architecture par Scarpa à l'architecture urbaine de la Vénétie. A titre d'exemple de ces phases d'évolution, il suffit de rappeler les projets réalisés par Scarpa dans les années cinquante, à savoir des bâtiments où les espaces ont des coins ouverts et vitrés. Outre le musée de Possagno, la Casa Veritti, à Udine, et quelques-uns des projets non réalisés – comme la Casa Zoppas à Conegliano et la Casa Taddei à Venise – sont de bons exemples de l'évolution de l'architecture de Scarpa. Il a rendu les fenêtres d'angle de la nouvelle conception spatiale dans le langage de la Vénétie: la lumière créée par ces fenêtres d'angle devient une clarté lumineuse chromatique résultant de transparences, qui a le caractère typique des œuvres plastiques de cette région depuis des siècles. Dans le pavillon du Vénézuela, sur le terrain de la Biennale à Venise, Scarpa a recouvert les fenêtres d'angle reliant les deux pièces d'exposition de grilles donnant de l'ombre qui rappellent d'autres solutions analogues choisies pour filtrer la lumière. Ses espaces naissent d'une lumineuse clarté qui, abstraction faite des évidentes différences de vocabulaire, produit les flots de lumière de Palladio et de l'architecture des XVIIe et XVIIIe siècles.

De cette manière, le langage architectonique de Scarpa lié à la Vénétie est enrichi d'autres éléments créatifs essentiels quand il passe des fenêtres d'angle ombragées au double revêtement de la façade que Louis Kahn et Robert Venturi ont à mon avis emprunté à l'architecture baroque.[16]

Scarpa a projeté pour la Banca Popolare di Verona des fenêtres qu'il avait vues des années auparavant dans un affreux bâtiment situé en face de l'hôtel Bristol, à Gênes, où il séjournait à cause de l'annexe prévue pour le Teatro di Genua. Les ouvertures nouvellement créées dans le revêtement extérieur de ce bâtiment avaient – et Scarpa attira mon attention là-dessus – une autre forme et étaient plus petites que les fenêtres du mur intérieur du bâtiment. Scarpa savait que la lumière reflétée par le verre serait de la sorte diffusée par la surface intérieure du revêtement extérieur, adoucissant ainsi l'effet de contre-jour tout en accroissant la luminosité de la pièce. Cette solution, qui se rapprochait encore davantage de l'architecture de Palladio et de la Vénétie – avec les surfaces stratifiées et transparentes –, permettait d'employer des fenêtres au milieu du mur sans occasionner de fâcheux effets éblouissants. Ce genre d'espace, dont le caractère est déterminé par le

Verkleidung – ein zentraler Aspekt meiner eigenen architektonischen Bemühungen – bestimmt wird, stellt ein äußerst wirkungsvolles Instrument dar, das typische Licht der Landschaft des Veneto und seiner Malerei zu erreichen, ein Licht, das zum Wesen der Natur und Kultur dieser Region gehört.[17]

Die Fähigkeit der Architektur, die Orte kenntlich zu machen, sie zum Sprechen zu bringen, indem sie sich in ihnen verwurzelt, diese Fähigkeit wird um so wichtiger, je mehr der internationale Kulturaustausch zunimmt. In diesem Zusammenhang ist die Rolle des Lichts von zentraler Bedeutung. Während ein im Internationalen Stil – und sei es auch in seiner postmodernen Version – ausgearbeiteter Entwurf ganz unabhängig von seinem Standort gesehen werden kann, kann ein Entwurf, der den Konsequenzen der Architektur für ihre Umgebung Rechnung trägt, nicht umhin, sich eben dort am Standort zu verwurzeln.

DIE ZEICHNUNG

Scarpa begann einen Entwurf, indem er Konfigurationen auswählte, die in seiner Arbeit immer wiederkehrten und die eine jeweils spezifische Bedeutung erhielten, wenn sie im Grundriß oder im Aufriß entsprechend angeordnet wurden, um syntaktisch genau bestimmte Funktionen im Gebäude zu erfüllen. Die Zeichnungen lassen die verschiedenen Versuche erkennen, Konfigurationen zu kombinieren, ebenso wie die schrittweisen Abänderungen in den Maßverhältnissen, die Scarpa als »Arbeit mit der Feile« bezeichnete. Alle diese Operationen haben im Prozeß des zeichnerischen Entwurfs ihre spezifische Struktur und wechseln die jeweils benutzte Unterlage: Transparentpapier, Karton, Reißbrett oder maßstabsgetreues Modell etc. Die Zeichnungen, die auf den auf dem Reißbrett befestigten Karton aufgetragen wurden, umfaßten den Gesamtkomplex – das ganze Gebäude zum Beispiel –, dieser entwickelte sich langsam und kumulativ, indem in ihn die nach und nach ausgearbeiteten Lösungsvorschläge für die verschiedenen Probleme eingingen. Diese Zeichnung auf dem Reißbrett blieb dann der Bezugsrahmen für die gesamte Arbeit von Anfang bis zum Abschluß des Entwurfs; häufig gab ein Lageplan den für den Eingriff vorgesehenen Standort wieder, einschließlich der Sektionen und Aufrisse, die direkt neben den Plan gezeichnet waren, soweit es die Größenverhältnisse des Eingriffs erlaubten.

Aus dieser umfassenden Zeichnung wurden die verschiedenen Probleme herausgelöst, um sie in einem anderen Maßstab zu bearbeiten; diese stellten auch die herausragenden formalen Ereignisse der Gestaltung dar. Die Zeichnungen, die in einem größeren Maßstab auf ockerfarbenem Karton entwickelt wurden, erlaubten eine eingehendere Behandlung des jeweiligen Pro-

double revêtement – un aspect essentiel de mes propres efforts architectoniques –, représente un instrument extrêmement efficace quand on veut obtenir la lumière typique du paysage de la Vénétie et de sa peinture, lumière qui fait partie de la nature et de la culture de cette région.[17]

L'architecture est capable de marquer les lieux, de les faire parler, en s'implantant dedans, et cette faculté est d'autant plus importante que les échanges culturels internationaux s'intensifient. A ce propos, le rôle de la lumière est d'une importance capitale. Alors qu'un projet élaboré dans le style international – même dans sa version postmoderne – peut être vu indépendamment de sa situation géographique, un projet, qui tient compte des conséquences que l'architecture a pour ses environs, ne peut s'empêcher de s'enraciner dans cet emplacement.

LE DESSIN

Scarpa commençait un projet en choisissant des configurations qui revenaient constamment dans son travail et qui avaient chaque fois une signification spécifique quand elles étaient arrangées au fur et à mesure sur le plan horizontal pour remplir dans le bâtiment une fonction exactement définie du point de vue de la syntaxe. Les dessins montrent les diverses tentatives entreprises pour combiner des configurations, ainsi que les modifications progressives dans les rapports dimensionnels, que Scarpa qualifiait de «fignolage». Toutes ces opérations ont leur structure spécifique dans le processus d'étude et changent respectivement de support: papier transparent, carton, planche à dessin ou maquette à l'échelle, etc.

Les dessins, qui avaient été exécutés sur le carton fixé sur la planche à dessin, comprenaient le complexe entier – tout le bâtiment par exemple –, celui-ci se développait lentement et de manière cumulative au fur et à mesure qu'arrivaient les propositions de solution élaborées pour les différents problèmes. Ce dessin sur la planche demeurait ensuite le cadre de référence pour l'ensemble du travail, du début à la fin du projet; un plan topographique reproduisait fréquemment l'emplacement prévu pour l'intervention, y compris les sections et les élévations qui étaient directement dessinées à côté du plan, dans la mesure où le permettaient les rapports de grandeur de l'intervention.

Les différents problèmes étaient détachés de ce vaste dessin afin d'être élaborés à une autre échelle; ceux-ci représentaient également les événements formels marquants de la conception. Les dessins, qui étaient développés à une plus grande échelle sur du carton ocre, permettaient un traitement plus détaillé du problème concerné et faisaient en outre l'objet de discussions avec des conseillers, des collaborateurs et des exécu-

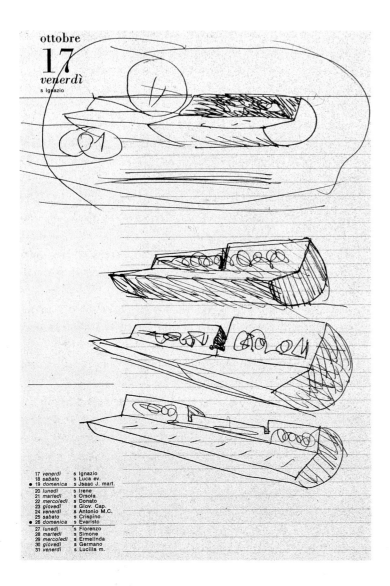

17 *venerdì*	s Ignazio	
18 *sabato*	s Luca ev.	
● 19 *domenica*	s Jsaac J. mart.	
20 *lunedì*	s Irene	
21 *martedì*	s Orsola	
22 *mercoledì*	s Donato	
23 *giovedì*	s Giov. Cap.	
24 *venerdì*	s Antonio M.C.	
25 *sabato*	s Crispino	
● 26 *domenica*	s Evaristo	
27 *lunedì*	s Fiorenzo	
28 *martedì*	s Simone	
29 *mercoledì*	s Ermelinda	
30 *giovedì*	s Germano	
31 *venerdì*	s Lucilla m.	

Brion Family Cemetery, San Vito d'Altivole, 1969–1978; sketches for the sarcophagi

nearer to Palladio and the Veneto, using stratified, transparent surfaces, allowed windows to be placed centrally in a wall while avoiding the concomitant effect of tiresome glare. Such a room, whose character is conditioned by its double skin – a central aspect of my own architectural explorations – most effectively achieves the typical light of the Veneto countryside and its paintings, a light which is central to the natural and cultural character of the region.[17]

This capacity of architecture to take root in places, and thereby bring out the genius loci and make it speak, is growing even more important with the increase in international exchanges. In this connection, the role of light is of paramount importance. While a design worked out in the international style – even in its postmodern manifestation – can be envisaged in isolation from its physical site, a design which takes account of the effect of architecture on its environment has no choice but to put down roots there.

THE DRAWING PROCESS

Scarpa began a design by using one of the configurations which constantly recur in his work, and which acquire a particular significance when inserted into a plan or elevation in order to fulfil syntactically defined functions in the building in question. The drawings reveal different attempts to combine these configurations, along with gradual changes in metric proportions which Scarpa referred to as »filing down«. All these operations in the design process were structured in a specific manner, while the actual medium was changed: tracing paper, cardboard, drawing-board, scale-model etc. The drawing on cardboard fixed to the drawing-board embraced the total complex – the whole building, for example – and developed slowly and cumulatively as the solutions worked out for various problems were filled in. This drawing-board version was the frame of reference for the whole project from start to finish.

From this comprehensive drawing, the individual problems were extracted to be tackled on a different scale; these constituted the chief formal events of the design process. These large-scale drawings on ochre-coloured card allowed a more in-depth study of the problem concerned, and were discussed with consultants and staff, as well as with the specialists and craftsmen who were to do the calculations or construct the individual elements, as the case might be.

Drafting a problem on card produced a certain organisational structure which followed the reference points of the project: axes, specifications where applicable, context-determined constraints etc. Using overlays of tracing paper, it was possible to try out variations on the theme drawn on the card. These variations con-

blems und waren darüber hinaus Gegenstand von Gesprächen mit Beratern, Mitarbeitern und Ausführenden, die die Berechnungen durchführen oder die einzelnen Komponenten bauen sollten.

Wenn das jeweilige Problem auf diesen Zeichenkarton aufgetragen wurde, dann ergab sich daraus eine bestimmte Organisationsstruktur, die die festen Bezugspunkte der vorgeschlagenen Konfiguration absteckte: die Achsen, die eventuellen Entwurfsvorgaben, die Zwänge des Kontextes etc. Nun konnte man auf Transparentpapier eine Reihe von Variationen zum Thema entwickeln, dessen Matrix sich auf dem Karton befand und an dessen durchscheinender Zeichnung man sich orientieren konnte. Die Variationen enthielten Vorschläge, die auf das als Grundlage dienende, gezeichnete Schema aufgetragen werden konnten und die wiederum in ihren jeweiligen Modifizierungen genau festgelegten Regeln folgten. Wurde einer der Lösungsvorschläge, die auf dem Transparentpapier entwickelt worden waren, als befriedigend beurteilt, dann wurde er auf den Karton übertragen. Wenn der Vorschlag als definitiv betrachtet wurde, konnte er auch auf dem Reißbrett gezeichnet werden, wo er den anderen, schon fertigen Teilen des Entwurfs und dem gesamten Kontext eingefügt wurde. Das aus dem Ganzen herausgelöste Problem zog seinerseits die Behandlung anderer Probleme nach sich, die in der gleichen Manier in Angriff genommen wurden.

In Scarpas kompositorischer Arbeit formalisierte der auf dem Reißbrett befestigte Karton das Anordnungsverfahren der ausgewählten Konfigurationen; der ockerfarbene Karton bestimmte gewissermaßen die Zerlegung der Arbeit in einzelne Formereignisse und folglich die syntaktische Organisation der Gesamtstruktur, während das Transparentpapier die Transformationsschritte im Entwurfsprozeß ermöglichte. Die Abfolge von schrittweisen und kontinuierlichen Variationen – erkennbar, wenn man die vielen Transparentpapiere, die dasselbe Thema behandeln, miteinander vergleicht – zeigen deutlich das Entstehen der kompositorischen Arbeit aus den ständigen Umgestaltungen; sie besitzen darüber hinaus einen argumentativen Charakter, der sie zu regelrecht bildnerischen Reflexionen werden läßt.

Diese Art der Zerlegung der Entwurfsarbeit in einzelne Formereignisse, die sich aus dem Gang der Konstruktion ergeben, könnte fälschlich den Eindruck eines parataktischen Charakters von Scarpas Arbeiten hervorrufen: Diese Episoden erscheinen tatsächlich wie Fragmente, aber sie sind solcher Art, daß sie ein Ganzes evozieren, dem sie entstammen. Wie in vielen Arbeiten der neuesten Architektur präsentieren sich die Figuren Scarpas vermittels einfacher Zeichen, Details, Bruchstücke, niemals jedoch vollständig. Und den-

tants qui devaient effectuer les calculs ou construire les différentes composantes.

Quand le problème concerné était porté sur ce carton à dessin, une certaine structure d'organisation, qui fixait les points de référence fixes de la configuration proposée – les axes, les éventuelles références d'étude, les contraintes du contexte, etc. – se dégageait. Il était alors possible de développer sur du papier transparent une série de variations relatives au thème, variations dont la matrice se trouvait sur le carton et dont le dessin translucide permettait de s'orienter. Ces variations renfermaient des propositions qui pouvaient être reportées sur le schéma dessiné servant de base et qui suivaient à leur tour des règles exactement fixées dans leurs modifications respectives. Quand l'une des solutions proposées, qui avaient été développées sur le papier transparent, était considérée comme satisfaisante, elle était alors reportée sur le carton. Quand la proposition était considérée comme définitive, elle pouvait également être dessinée sur la planche à dessin où elle était insérée dans les autres parties déjà terminées du projet et dans tout le contexte. Le problème détaché du tout permettait de son côté de traiter d'autres problèmes, auxquels on s'attaquait ensuite de la même manière.

Dans le travail structurel de Scarpa, le carton fixé sur la planche à dessin réduisait le système de disposition des configurations choisies à ses structures formelles; le carton ocre déterminait en quelque sorte la décomposition du travail en événements formels individuels et, par conséquent, l'organisation syntaxique de la structure globale, tandis que le papier transparent rendait possible les étapes de transformation dans le procédé d'étude. La suite de variations progressives et permanentes – reconnaissables, quand on compare entre eux les nombreux papiers transparents qui traitent le même thème – montre nettement la naissance du travail structurel à partir des transformations constantes; elles possèdent en outre un caractère dialectique, qui les transforme en réflexions vraiment créatives.

Cette manière de décomposer le travail de projection en événements formels isolés résultant de la marche de la construction pourrait à tort donner l'impression que les œuvres de Scarpa ont un caractère paratactique: ces épisodes font effectivement figure de fragments, mais ils sont tels qu'il évoquent un tout dont ils sont issus. Comme dans de nombreuses œuvres de l'architecture la plus récente, les figures de Scarpa se présentent sous forme de simples dessins, détails et fragments, mais jamais complètement. Et pourtant, elles renvoient à des complexes auxquels elles sont virtuellement liées, si bien que l'on sent intuitivement les pénétrations, les chevauchements et les entrelacements qui annoncent une disposition hypotactique. Dans l'architecture de Scarpa, on ne trouve guère le genre de juxtaposition de

Brion Family Cemetery, San Vito d'Altivole,
1969–1978; design and execution of the
chapel roof

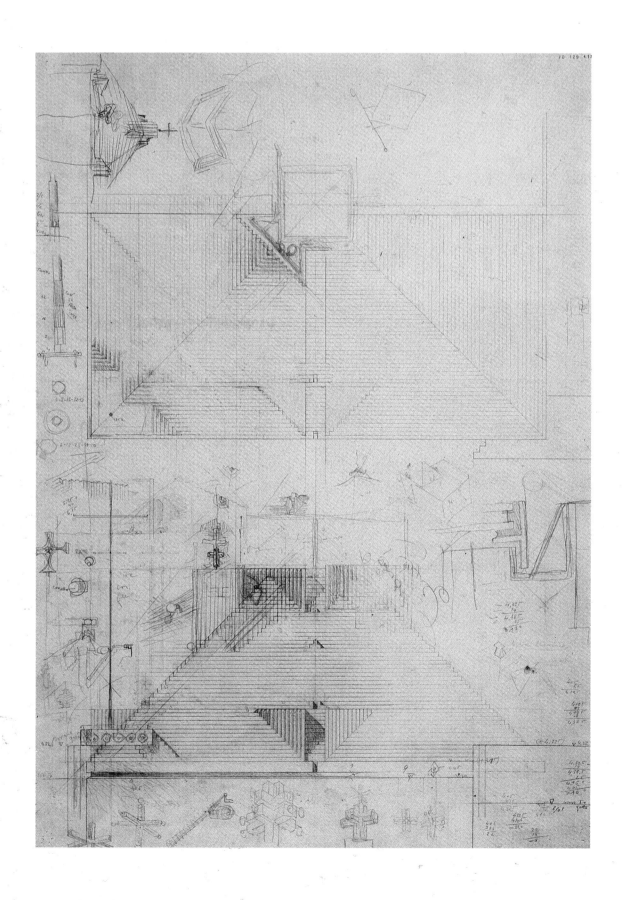

tained proposals which could be inserted into the base drawing to become, in their turn, modified by set procedures. When a variant on tracing-paper was considered satisfactory, it was transferred to the drawing-board and inserted into the completed parts of the total design. A problem thus abstracted from the whole necessitated the treatment of other problems, which were then tackled along the same lines.

In Scarpa's composition work, the card drawing on the drawing-board formalised the allocation of the selected configurations; the ochre-card drawing defined the dissection of the work into specific formal events, and thus the syntactic organisation of the system, while the tracing-paper put into effect the transformations characteristic of Scarpa's design procedure. The sequence of continuous gradual change – seen on comparing the many tracing-paper versions – shows clearly how the composition evolved; moreover, they have an argumentative character, transforming them into true figurative inferences.

This way of splitting the design process into formal events resulting from the construction operations could give the false impression that Scarpa's method was paratactic. While these episodes do indeed appear as fragments, they are such as to evoke the totality from which they proceed. As in much recent architecture, Scarpa's shapes are manifested in simple signs, details and fragments – never as complete units. And yet they point to complexes to which they are virtually linked, so that one senses interpenetrations, overlaps and intertwinings which hint at an underlying hypotactic structure. In Scarpa's architecture it is difficult to find the juxtaposition of clearly defined volumes typical of the paratactic design procedure of the Neoclassicists. In connection with rules of proportion and scale which accompanied and conrolled the »filing down«, mention should be made of Scarpa's interest in the geometrical conundrums of Mathila Ghyka. One can see how in his last projects, such as the Banca Popolare di Verona, when he was moving towards what might be calles a regionalist grammar, he was reverting to a Classical architectural system, although this had more to do with the hypotactic mode of the Baroque or of Mannerism than with the paratactic character of Neoclassicism.[18] If we recognize the Veneto ingredient in Scarpa's architecture, we should refer to the special qualities of Venetian classicism, which, unlike Alberti, Bramante or Brunelleschi, never relied on composition with three-dimensional cells. Rather, he goes back to Serlio, Sanmicheli, Sansovino, Palladio, Scamozzi etc., with their transparent shapes and stratifications, seem to me to explain much of the complexity of Carlo Scarpa's architecture.

noch verweisen sie auf Komplexe, mit denen sie virtuell verbunden sind, so daß man Durchdringungen, Überlappungen und Verflechtungen, die eine hypotaktische Anordnung erahnen lassen intuitiv spürt. Man findet in der Architektur Scarpas kaum jene Art der Juxtaposition von sauber definierten Baukörpern, die die parataktische Gestaltungsordnung des Neoklassizismus kennzeichnet.

Was die Regeln der Proportionierung und der Dimensionierung betrifft, die seine »Feilarbeit« begleiteten und orientierten, so ist sein Interesse für die geometrischen Spiele von Mathila Ghyka zu erwähnen. Man kann beobachten, daß Scarpa sich in seinen letzten Projekten, etwa bei der Banca Popolare di Verona, als er sich einer Grammatik näherte, die man regionalistisch nennen könnte, dem klassischen Architektursystem wieder zuwandte, dabei jedoch mehr dem hypotaktischen Modus des Barock und des Manierismus verpflichtet war als dem parataktischen Charakter des Neoklassizismus.[18] Erkennt man den dem Veneto verbundenen Charakter der Architektur Scarpas, dann muß man auf die Besonderheit des venetischen Klassizismus verweisen, der nie wie bei Alberti, Brunelleschi oder Bramante auf der Komposition von dreidimensionalen Zellen beruhte. Er geht vielmehr zurück auf Serlio, Sanmicheli, Sansovino, Palladio, Scamozzi u.a., die meines Erachtens mit ihren transparenten Formen und Stratifizierungen viele Seiten der Komplexität von Scarpas Architektursprache erklären.

corps nettement définis qui caractérise les créations paratactiques du Néo-classicisme.

En ce qui concerne les règles des proportions et des dimensions, qui accompagnaient et orientaient son «fignolage», il convient de mentionner son intérêt pour les jeux géométriques de Mathola Ghyka. On peut observer que dans ses derniers projets, par exemple la Banca Popolare di Verona, Scarpa s'est approché d'une grammaire que l'on pourrait qualifier de régionaliste et s'est de nouveau tourné vers le système architectonique classique, tout en étant davantage tenu au mode hypotactique du Baroque et du Maniérisme qu'à la nature paratactique du Néo-classicisme.[18] Si l'on reconnaît que l'architecture de Scarpa est liée à la Vénétie, il faut alors signaler la particularité du Classicisme vénitien qui ne reposait jamais sur la composition de cellules tridimensionnelles comme chez Alberti, Brunelleschi ou Bramante. Il remonte au contraire à Serlio, Sanmicheli, Sansovino, Palladio, Scamozzi, etc. qui, avec leurs formes et leurs stratifications transparentes, expliquent à mon avis de nombreux aspects de la complexité du langage architectonique de Scarpa.

1 In his lectures and in the field Scarpa often described the dissociation of elements as his basic mode of approach in designing, cf. my monograph on Scarpa: *Carlo Scarpa. Architetto Poeta* (Venice 1967). As to the poetic side of his fragments, cf. Tafuri, »Il frammento, la ›figura‹, il gioco. Carlo Scarpa e la cultura italiana« in F. Dal Co, Mazzariol, G., *Carlo Scarpa. Opera completa.* Milan 1984.

2 Novalis maintained that in his opinion one should transcend many stages to perfect creation, and to be a writer one should spend a period as a teacher and as an artisan.

3 Los, S., *Carlo Scarpa. Architetto Poeta*, op.cit.

4 Junod, P., *Trasparence e opacitè.* Lausanne 1976.

5 Dal Co, F., »›Genie ist Fleiß.‹ L'architettura di Carlo Scarpa« in *Carlo Scarpa. Opera completa,* op. cit.

6 Heidegger, M., *Die Kunst und der Raum.* St Gallen 1969.

7 Heidegger, M., *Der Ursprung des Kunstwerks.* Frankfurt am Main 1950.

8 Benjamin, W., *Der Begriff der Kunstkritik in der deutschen Romantik.* Frankfurt am Main 1973.

9 Goodman, N., *Sprachen der Kunst.* Frankfurt am Main 1973.

10 The contextual character of works of art and architecture is discussed in H.-G. Gadamer, *Wahrheit und Methode.* Tübingen 1990.

11 An essay which provides a commentary on Semper's theories is to be found in Fiedler, K., *Essay on Architecture.* Lexington, KY. 1954

12 Von Meiss, P., *Elements of Architecture.* London 1990.

13 Zevi, B., *Poetica dell'architettura neoplastica.* Milan 1953; Godoli, E., *Jan Wils, Frank Lloyd Wright and De Stijl.* Florence 1980.

14 Wright, F. Lloyd , »The Destruction of the Box« in Kaufmann, E., *An American Architecture.* New York 1955.

15 Reichlin, B., »Le Corbusier e De Stijl« in *Casabella* N., pp. 520–1. Milan 1986.

16 Los, S., »Multi-Scale Architecture« in Hawkes, D., Owers, J., Rickaby, P., Steadman, P. (eds.), *Energy and Urban Built Form.* London 1987.

17 Los, S., »Disegni e costruzioni di architettura« in *Parametro* N.174, September – October 1989, numero monografico.

18 For Tafuri, Scarpa's work pursues a poetry of shapes; he discusses the dialectic between form and shape, between form and image, in connection with the transition from Mannerism to the Baroque in his essay »Le strutture del linguaggio nella storia dell'architettura moderna« in Samona, G. (curator), *Teorie della progettazione architettonica.* Bari 1968.

SELECTED BUILDINGS AND PROJECTS

Apart from museum architecture, exhibition design – temporary architecture – was a central element in Scarpa's work. His exhibition designs could be seen in Milan, Turin, Rome, London, Paris, and – above all – time and again in Venice. In 1972, with his show »Aspects of Modern Italian Sculpture«, he ended thirty years of cooperation with the Venice Biennale. The main intention of his exhibition work was to take over the »language« of the works on display and to »speak« the same way in his design. He aimed at an amplification which in no small way enhanced an understanding of the exhibits.

Scarpa's tool for discovery was drawing; his tool for communication was architecture. His ability to exhibit art in a charismatic, fascinating way thus comes as no surprise. What art critics say in words, Scarpa said in space, surface, colour and light. The interrelations he created between the exhibits and architecture were true »labels« of his achievement. Just as he could not design a house without knowing where it was to be built, he could not design an exhibition room without knowing what was to be displayed. The two aspects are connected by the idea of always concentrating on dialogue, avoiding the expression of one's personal intuitions in isolation.

Scarpa never simply hung a ready-framed picture on the wall; he always thought up three-dimensional designs specially for the work concerned. Light is always fundamental: often it is adjusted with great sensitivity; sometimes it is brutal, achieving effects which do not simply display something but prescribe a certain path, certain interruptions or vetoes for the eye. Light and colour are not neutral; they are commentators, explaining, interpreting and describing. Scarpa's exhibitions were never boring.

»Florentine Frescoes« exhibition, London, 1969 (left page); »The Sense of Colour and the Rule of the Waters« exhibition, Turin, 1961 (below)

»Frank Lloyd Wright« exhibition, Milan, 1960
(above); exhibit design for the Venice Biennale,
1962 (below)

Neben der Einrichtung von Museen gehört die
Ausstellungsgestaltung – eine Architektur auf
Zeit – zu den zentralen Bereichen in Scarpas
Werk. Seine Installationen waren in Mailand,
Turin, Rom, London, Paris und vor allem immer wieder in Venedig zu sehen. Mit einer
Ausstellung zum Thema »Aspekte der italienischen Skulptur der Gegenwart« schloß er
1972 schließlich seine dreißigjährige Mit-
arbeit an der Biennale von Venedig ab. Lei-
tender Gedanke seiner Ausstellungspraxis
war, die »Sprache« der ausgestellten Kunstwerke zu übernehmen und Ausstattungen zu
entwerfen, die dieselbe Sprache sprechen. Es
ging ihm um eine Amplifikation, eine Verstär-
kung, die ganz wesentlich zum Verständnis
der Exponate beitrug. Man ist deshalb von seiner Fähigkeit, Kunstwerke auf charismatische
und faszinierende Weise auszustellen, nicht
überrascht.

Scarpas Erkenntnisinstrument war die architektonische Zeichnung, Kommunikationsin-
strument die Architektur. Das, was der Kunst-
kritiker mit Worten ausdrückt, artikulierte
Scarpa mit dem Raum, den Flächen, der Farbe
und mit Licht. Wesentliches Kennzeichen seiner Arbeit waren die Wechselbeziehungen,
die er zwischen dem Werk und der Architektur herstellte. So wie er kein Haus planen
konnte, ohne zu wissen, wo es gebaut werden
sollte, so konnte er auch keine Einrichtung
planen, ohne zu wissen, welchen Kunstwerken sie dienen sollte. Beide Aspekte sind miteinander verbunden durch die Auffassung,
immer in einem Kontext zu arbeiten, die eigenen persönlichen Intuitionen nicht isoliert
auszudrücken, sondern sich auf den Dialog
zu konzentrieren.

Man wird bei Scarpa nie ein gerahmtes Bild
antreffen, das er beziehungslos an die Wand
gehängt hätte; vielmehr gibt es immer drei-
dimensionale Kontexte, die für die Objekte
gestaltet sind. Das Licht spielt dabei eine fun-
damentale Rolle: Häufig wird es mit großer
Sensibilität reguliert, manchmal geradezu
brutal eingesetzt, um Wirkungen zu erzielen,
die nicht einfach etwas vorzeigen wollen,
sondern die dem Auge einen bestimmten
Weg, eine bestimmte Unterbrechung vor-
schreiben, auch Verbote auferlegen. Licht
und Farbe kommentieren durchaus nicht neutral, sie erklären, interpretieren, beschreiben.
Jedenfalls sind Scarpas Einrichtungen niemals
langweilig.

En plus de l'aménagement de musées, l'installation d'expositions – une architecture limitée dans le temps – fait partie des principaux domaines de l'œuvre de Scarpa. On a pu voir ses installations à Milan, à Turin, à Rome, à Londres, Paris et surtout à plusieurs reprises à Venise. En 1972, il mit fin à trente ans de collaboration à la Biennale de Venise avec une exposition sur le thème «Aspects de la sculpture italienne du présent». L'idée dominante de sa pratique des expositions était de reprendre le «langage» des œuvres d'art exposées et de réaliser des décorations parlant le même langage. Il s'agissait pour lui d'une amplification, d'une intensification qui entrait pour beaucoup dans la compréhension des œuvres d'art exposées.

L'instrument de la connaissance de Scarpa était le dessin d'architecture, son instrument de communication était l'architecture. Il n'est donc pas surprenant qu'il ait pu exposer des œuvres d'art d'une manière à la fois charismatique et fascinante. Ce que le critique d'art exprime avec des mots, Scarpa l'articulait avec l'espace, les surfaces, la couleur et la lumière. Son travail était avant tout caractérisé par les corrélations qu'il créait entre l'œuvre et l'architecture. De même qu'il ne pouvait concevoir une maison sans savoir où elle serait construite, il ne pouvait pas concevoir une installation sans savoir à quelles œuvres d'art elle devrait servir. Les deux aspects sont liés par l'idée de toujours travailler dans un contexte, de ne pas exprimer les intuitions personnelles de manière isolée, mais de se concentrer sur le dialogue.

On ne rencontrera jamais chez Scarpa un tableau encadré qu'il aurait simplement accroché au mur, il y a au contraire toujours des contextes tridimensionnels conçus pour les objets. La lumière joue un rôle fondamental: souvent, elle est réglée avec une grande sensibilité; quelquefois, elle est brutalement mise à contribution pour obtenir des effets qui ne veulent pas simplement montrer quelque chose, mais imposent à l'œil un chemin précis, des interruptions fixées et même des interdits. La lumière et la couleur ne commentent pas d'une manière neutre, elles expliquent, interprètent et décrivent. En tout cas, les installations de Scarpa ne sont jamais ennuyeuses.

»Vitality in Art« exhibition, Venice, 1959 (above); exhibit design for the Venice Biennale, 1972 (below)

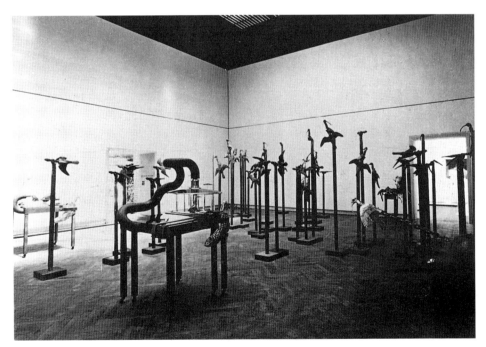

VILLA ZOPPAS

Conegliano, Treviso, 1953
In collaboration with: P. Celotto

Scarpa designed several versions of this house, which was never built. Perhaps because they stayed on paper, these drafts, more than others, were preoccupied with Frank Lloyd Wright's theories. In this important creative period Scarpa was aiming for continuity in space, with supports and walls used as plastic objects creating inside and outside space. Right-angled layouts alternate with hexagonal ones, resulting in complex spatial situations, which would be most interesting when built.

At first the plan developed around a central element, the reference point for the design of the other spaces, the cruciform layout which distinguishes several of Wright's houses. A later version would provide for tall supports as fixed points for the roof, in a manner that owned much to De Stijl. In the final versions the composition was more compact and sober, possibly because the project was finally approaching realisation after lengthy work on the drawing board.

These experiments in composition were only partly inspired by the commission and show Scarpa's interest in theory, which found expression in drawing.

Scarpa erarbeitete mehrere Entwürfe für dieses Haus, das jedoch nie realisiert wurde. Stärker als in anderen Fällen, vielleicht weil sie auf dem Papier geblieben sind, sind die Entwürfe für die Villa Zoppas Ergebnis seiner Beschäftigung mit den Themen Frank Lloyd Wrights. Das Bemühen um räumliche Kontinuität, bei dem die Stützen und Wände zu plastischen Objekten werden, die Innen- und Außenräume schaffen, sind kennzeichnende Momente dieser wichtigen Schaffensperiode von Scarpa. Orthogonale Anordnungen wechseln mit hexagonalen, woraus komplexe Raumsituationen entstehen, deren Rekonstruktion sehr interessant wäre.

Ursprünglich entwickelte sich der Plan um ein zentrales Element, das Bezugspunkt wurde für die Gestaltung der anderen Räume – Scarpa übernimmt hier das kreuzförmige Motiv, das viele Häuser Wrights bestimmt. In einer späteren Fassung waren hohe Stützen vorgesehen, die nach einem dem De Stijl verpflichteten Plan als Fixpunkte der Dachkonstruktion dienten. In den letzten Versionen wurde die Komposition dann wieder kompakter und nüchterner, vielleicht weil das Ganze sich nach langer Projektierungsarbeit nun der Realisationsphase näherte.

Solche kompositorischen Experimente waren nur zum Teil vom Auftrag her motiviert und zeigen Scarpas Interesse an einer theoretischen Reflexion, die sich im Zeichnen vollzieht.

Scarpa élabora plusieurs plans pour cette maison qui ne fut pourtant jamais réalisée. Plus encore que dans d'autres cas, peut-être parce qu'ils sont restés couchés sur le papier, ces plans sont le résultat de sa confrontation avec les thèmes de Frank Lloyd Wright. L'effort de continuité spatiale, au cours duquel les supports et les murs se transforment en objets plastiques créant des pièces intérieures et extérieures, est le facteur caractéristique de cette importante période créatrice de Scarpa. Des arrangements orthogonaux alternent avec des arrangements hexagonaux, ce qui donne naissance à des situations spatiales complexes qu'il serait très intéressant de reconstruire. Scarpa imagina d'abord le plan autour d'un élément central qui devint le point de référence pour la réalisation des autres pièces – c'est le motif en forme de croix qui détermine de nombreuses maisons de Wright. Dans une version ultérieure, on avait prévu de hauts supports qui représentaient les points fixes d'après un plan devant beaucoup au mouvement De Stijl, points fixes pour la construction du toit. Dans les dernières versions, la composition devint plus compacte et plus sobre, peut-être parce que l'ensemble s'approchait désormais de la phase de réalisation, au bout d'un long travail de projection.

Les expériences structurelles de ce genre étaient seulement en partie motivées par la commande et montrent l'intérêt que Scarpa portait à la réflexion théorique qui s'accomplit dans le dessin.

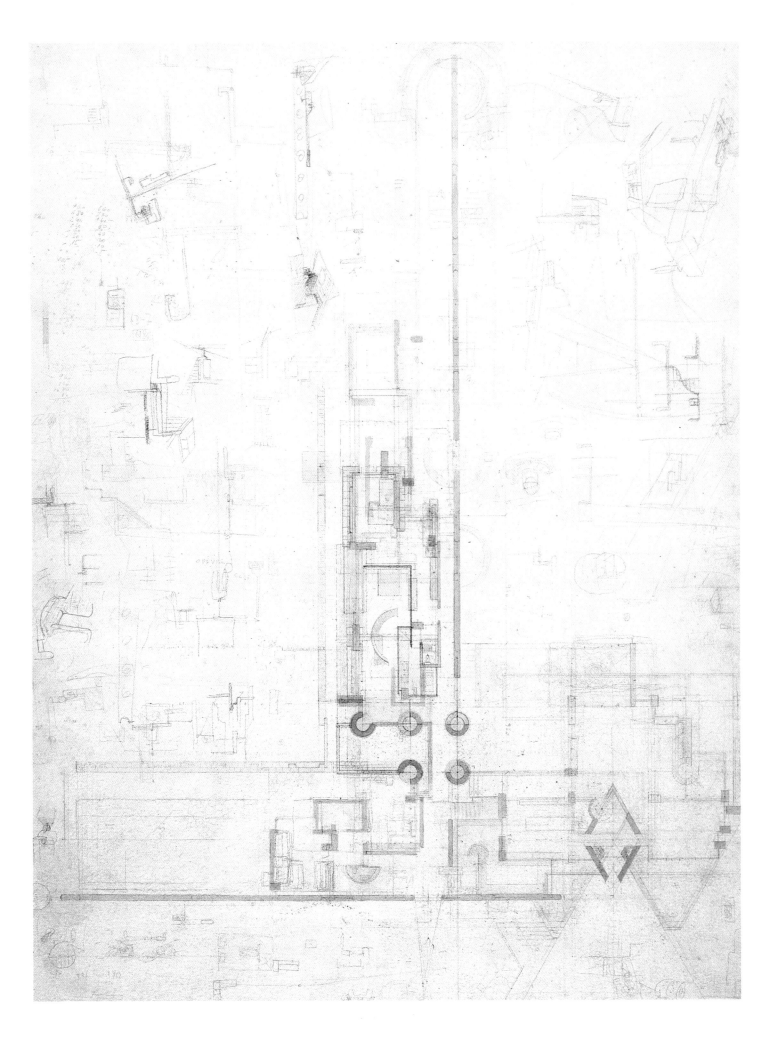

GIPSOTECA CANOVIANA

Possagno, Treviso, 1955–1957
In collaboration with: V. Pastor

In 1955, to commemorate the two hundredth anniversary of the birth of Antonio Canova, Carlo Scarpa was asked to extend the Canova Museum at Possagno, so as to rehouse the artist's copies, original plaster casts, marble sculptures and terracotta designs, which till then had been too tightly crammed together. The existing basilica-plan building, erected by Giuseppe Segusini between 1831 and 1836, was one of the first structures to be designed specifically as a museum.

The elongated site available to Scarpa, in a road sloping down the valley, was not large. Scarpa built the roof to resemble a waterfall that originates at the top of the hall running down between two converging walls and ending with a glass wall facing a pool of water. He thus multiplied the possible views and placed the sculptures in such a way as to strengthen the contrast between the abstract white of the plaster and the vital realism of the recumbent or upright female bodies. In this connection Scarpa spoke of a frame effect. At the far end of the long extension, where the water surface ruffled by the wind reflects a shimmering light, Scarpa placed the group of the Three Graces. This hesitant brilliance, so to speak, interprets well the mythical femininity of the dancing girls.

To achieve a well-modulated, varied light in the room, Scarpa consciously arranged for openings where the walls joined, creating corner windows. The light is thus always thrown onto a vertical diffusing surface, appreciably reducing the glare of normal windows. But there was another curious result: »I wanted to cut up the blue of the sky«, commented Scarpa.

Anläßlich des 200. Geburtstages von Antonio Canova wurde Carlo Scarpa 1955 mit der Erweiterung des Canova-Museums in Possagno beauftragt. Dort sollte Raum geschaffen werden, um Original-Gipsabgüsse des Künstlers, Kopien, einige Marmorplastiken und Entwürfe aus Terracotta unterzubringen, die in der bisherigen Präsentation allzusehr zusammengedrängt standen. Das schon vorhandene basilikaartige Gebäude, von Giuseppe Segusini zwischen 1831 und 1836 errichtet, gehört zu den ersten ausdrücklich als Museum geplanten Bauten.

Der Scarpa zur Verfügung stehende Baugrund, von länglicher Form und bescheidenen Ausmaßen, befindet sich an einer zum Tal hin abfallenden Straße. Scarpa baute ein Kaskadendach, das, ausgehend von einem hochgelegenen Saal, die stufenweise abfallenden Ebenen des konisch zulaufenden Raumes aufgreift und über einer Glaswand mit vorgelagertem Wasserbecken endet. Damit vervielfältigte er die Blickpunkte und situierte die Skulpturen so, daß der Kontrast zwischen dem abstrakten Weiß des Gipses und dem lebendigen Realismus der liegenden oder aufrecht stehenden Frauenkörper hervortritt. Scarpa sprach in diesem Zusammenhang von einem Rahmeneffekt. Am äußersten Ende des langgestreckten Neubaus, dort, wo die Wasserfläche des vorgelagerten Beckens ein flimmerndes, lebendiges Licht zurückwirft, regelrecht die Vibration der vom Wind gekräuselten Fläche weitergibt, plazierte Scarpa die Figurengruppe der drei Grazien. Die sozusagen zögernde Helligkeit interpretiert besser als jeder andere Kommentar die mythische Weiblichkeit dieser tanzenden Mädchen.

Zur Herstellung eines artikulierten, variationsreichen Raumlichts verwendete Scarpa vor allem gezielt gesetzte Öffnungen, für deren Gestaltung er Wandverbindungen so ausschnitt, daß sich Fenster-Eckkörper ergaben. Bei dieser Lösung trifft das Licht immer auf eine senkrechte Verteilerfläche, der Blendungseffekt wird, verglichen mit herkömmlichen Fenstern, deutlich reduziert; außerdem erzielt diese Lösung ein außergewöhnliches Ergebnis: »Ich wollte das Blau des Himmels zerschneiden«, kommentierte Scarpa selbst.

A l'occasion du 200e anniversaire d'Antonio Canova, en 1955, Carlo Scarpa fut chargé d'agrandir le Musée Canova à Possagno. Il s'agissait de caser les plâtres originaux de l'artiste, des copies, quelques statues en marbre et études en terre cuite qui étaient trop serrés les uns contre les autres dans l'ancienne présentation. Le bâtiment existant en forme de basilique, qui avait été construit entre 1831 et 1836 par Giuseppe Segusini, fait partie des premiers bâtiments conçus comme musées.

Le terrain à bâtir de forme allongée et de dimensions restreintes mis à la disposition de Scarpa est situé dans une rue qui descend en pente vers la vallée. Scarpa a construit un toit en cascade qui part d'une salle située en hauteur, reprend les niveaux progressivement inclinés de la pièce en forme de cône et prend fin au-dessus d'un mur vitré avec un bassin à eau situé devant. Il a ainsi multiplié les points de vue et situé les sculptures pour faire ressortir le contraste entre le blanc abstrait des plâtres et le réalisme vivant des corps féminins couchés ou debout. Scarpa a parlé à ce propos d'effet-cadre. A l'extrémité de l'annexe allongée, là où la surface de l'eau du bassin situé devant le mur renvoie une lumière scintillante pleine de vie et transmet effectivement la vibration de la surface ridée par le vent, Scarpa a placé le groupe des Trois Grâces. La clarté pour ainsi dire hésitante interprète mieux que tout autre commentaire la féminité mythique de ces jeunes femmes en train de danser.

Afin de créer une lumière articulée et riche en variations, Scarpa a avant tout utilisé des ouvertures placées méthodiquement et pour la création desquelles il a découpé des liaisons murales de façon à créer des fenêtres d'angle. Dans cette solution, la lumière rencontre toujours une surface de distribution verticale, et l'effet d'éblouissement est nettement réduit par rapport aux fenêtres ordinaires; elle a en outre un résultat extraordinaire: «Je voulais découper le bleu du ciel», a dit Scarpa.

Carlo Scarpa's extension: In the left foreground
»Recumbent Magdalena«, in the centre »Dirce«,
in the background the »Three Graces«, to the
right, on the wall, the relief »Socrates' Apology«

Previous page: The old Canova Museum by
Giuseppe Segusini

261 GEORGE WASHINGTON

»Sleeping Nymph«, behind, a bust of Napoleon,
in the glass case the terracotta of Princess Leopoldina
Esterhàzy

Opposite page, from left to right: George Washington
in the costume of a Roman General, a monument
for the State Capitol in Raleigh, North Carolina, a bust
of Canova, »Naiads«, bozzetto for the tombstone of
Pope Clement XIV, »Amor and Psyche with Butterfly«

South side of the extension (below); the »Three Graces« (right page)

Of the two long walls which form the new extension, the solid windowless outer wall on the side towards the road reflects the light back into the display area, providing an appropriate background for the contours of the sculptures. The second wall, parallel to the existing museum, allows for a narrow path between the old and the new building. Its front part is a steel frame filled with glass or soft Vicenza stone with »peephole« windows. Each statue is specially placed for the space and the light it needs, which may be glaring or else gently caresses the plaster-casts, giving them various appearances with the changes of the day, the season or the weather. Giuseppe Mazzariol therefore speaks of »actors in stone«; the visitor has the impression of sharing the lives of these sculptures.

For the wall plaster, Scarpa said his first spontaneous idea was for a deep black background for the pale sculptures. But pondering the effect of this contrast on the adjacent hall where the walls were all painted grey, Scarpa decided to keep the unexpected play of white against white we now take so much for granted. The old part of the building was later painted white, too.

The internal walls are smoothly plastered with a mixture of slaked lime, powdered marble and water. The more external walls are plastered with »graniglia« of grit, cement and Bologna plaster.

Von den beiden langen Wänden, die den neuen Teil des Museums im wesentlichen bilden, reflektiert die massive, geschlossene Mauer, die das Gebäude zur Straße hin begrenzt, das Licht in den Ausstellungsraum und verleiht ihm – als angemessenen Hintergrund für die Skulpturen – entsprechende Kontur. Die zweite Wand ist parallel zum schon vorhandenen Museum angelegt worden und ließ einen schmalen Weg zwischen Alt- und Neubau entstehen. Im vorderen Teil ist sie großflächig verglast, im hinteren Teil als Fläche aus weichem Vicenza-Stein mit kleindimensionierten »Einblicken« ausgeführt.

Jedes Exponat hat seinen sehr bestimmten Ort, sowohl hinsichtlich des Raums als auch hinsichtlich des Lichts, das die Kunstwerke manchmal kraß, manchmal mild und nuanciert modelliert und sie im Verlaufe des Tages, der Jahreszeiten, der Wetterveränderungen immer wieder anders erscheinen läßt. Aus diesem Grunde sprach Giuseppe Mazzariol von »steinernen Personen«: Der Betrachter hat das Gefühl, mit diesen Wesen zusammenzuleben.

Was den Verputz angehe, so erzählte Scarpa, habe er zunächst spontan daran gedacht, für die hellen Skulpturen einen tiefschwarzen Hintergrund zu wählen. Doch angesichts der Wirkung eines solchen Kontrastes auf den angrenzenden Raum, in dem alle Wände grau gestrichen waren, entschied sich Scarpa, es bei dem unerwarteten Spiel von Weiß auf Weiß zu belassen, das uns jetzt als eine solche Selbstverständlichkeit erscheint. Daraufhin wurde auch der alte Teil des Museums weiß gestrichen.

Die Innenwände sind mit einer Mischung aus Löschkalk, pulverisiertem Marmor, Kleister und Wasser gespachtelt, die Außenwände mit einer »graniglia« aus Grieß, Zement und Bologna-Gips verputzt.

Deux longs murs forment en substance la nouvelle partie du musée du plâtre. Le mur extérieur, massif et fermé du côté de la rue, reflète la lumière dans la salle d'exposition et lui donne, comme arrière-plan approprié aux sculptures, le contour correspondant. Le second mur est placé parallèlement au musée existant et crée un étroit chemin entre l'ancienne et la nouvelle construction. Dans la partie avant, c'est une grande surface vitrée, dans la partie arrière, c'est une surface en pierre tendre de Vicence avec des «vues» de petites dimensions.

Chaque statue a un emplacement très précis, aussi bien par rapport à l'espace que par rapport à la lumière, qui modèle les moulages en plâtre exposés d'une manière parfois brutale, parfois douce et nuancée, les fait paraître toujours différents au cours de la journée et des saisons, selon les conditions météorologiques. Pour cette raison, Giuseppe Mazzariol a parlé de «personnes en pierre»: le spectateur a l'impression de vivre avec ces êtres.

Pour ce qui est du crépi, Scarpa a raconté qu'il avait spontanément songé à choisir un arrière-plan d'un noir profond pour les sculptures. Mais, étant donné l'effet produit par un pareil contraste sur l'espace avoisinant, dans lequel tous les murs étaient peints en gris, Scarpa avait décidé d'en rester au jeu inattendu du blanc sur blanc qui nous semble maintenant naturel. Sur ce, l'ancienne partie du musée fut également peinte en blanc.

Les murs intérieurs sont badigeonnés avec un mélange de chaux éteinte, de marbre pulvérisé, de colle d'amidon et d'eau; les murs qui sont davantage tournés vers l'extérieur ont été crépis avec une «graniglia» faite de gravier, de ciment et de plâtre de Bologne.

Corner window in the extension by Carlo Scarpa

CASA VERITTI

Udine, 1955–1961
In collaboration with: C. Maschietto,
F. Marconi, A. Morelli

Carlo Scarpa received this commission from the lawyer Luigi Veritti, a relation of Angelo Masieri, who shared Scarpa's interest in the architecture of Frank Lloyd Wright. The plot recommended by Scarpa was in a relatively undeveloped area, but the client decided on a long, narrow site on the edge of Udine. The project involved two main problems: first the long, narrow site and secondly the characterless district, neither town nor country, with a few detached houses, typical of the outskirts of a modern town.

On restricted sites, Scarpa liked curved structures. »One can have narrow passages as long as they widen at the end, and that is achieved with curved walls«, he said. To avoid having a plan with right angles conditioned by the shape of the site, Scarpa drew a plan with two circles. But as the design developed, the second circle declined in importance and became a conservatory; the client wanted a more compact house which would therefore have to be on two storeys. But this attempt to harmonize the ideas of the architect with the wishes of the client also came to nothing. The differing building elements accumulated, culminating in a single building enclosed in a semicircular wall protecting the house like a snail shell to the north, while remaining quite open to the south to let the sun in and point the house towards a less populous area.

Carlo Scarpa erhielt diesen Auftrag von dem Rechtsanwalt Luigi Veritti, einem Verwandten von Angelo Masieri, mit dem Scarpa das Interesse für die Architektur Frank Lloyd Wrights teilte. Das Baugelände, das Scarpa empfohlen hatte, befand sich in einem wenig bebauten Gebiet. Der Bauherr jedoch entschied sich für ein langes, schmales Grundstück an der Peripherie von Udine. Für den Entwurf stellten sich damit im wesentlichen zwei Probleme: erstens die längliche Form des Grundstücks und zweitens der amorphe Charakter des Wohngebiets, nicht mehr freie Natur und doch noch nicht Stadt, zersiedelt von einzelnen Gebäuden – die typische Landschaft an der Peripherie heutiger Städte.

Bei besonders engen räumlichen Bedingungen neigte Scarpa zu gekurvten Konstruktionen. »Man kann durchaus auch enge Durchgänge haben, wenn sich nur dann der Raum wieder weitet,˙ und das erreicht man, wenn man die Wände krümmt«, sagte er. Um zu vermeiden, daß der Grundriß mit orthogonalen Anordnungen die strenge Rechtwinkligkeit des Grundstücks wiederholt, entwarf Scarpa einen Plan, dem eine Anordnung der Baukörper in Form von zwei Kreisen zugrunde lag. Doch im weiteren Verlauf der Arbeit verlor der zweite Kreis zunehmend an Bedeutung und wurde zu einem Wintergarten; da der Auftraggeber einem kompakteren Gebäude mit zwei Stockwerken den Vorzug gab. Doch auch diese Vorschläge, die die Vorstellungen des Architekten und die Wünsche des Auftraggebers miteinander zu vereinbaren suchten, wurden nicht umgesetzt. Die bisher unterschiedenen Bauelemente überlagern sich nun und bestimmen einen einzigen Baukörper, der von einer halbzylindrischen Mauer umschlossen ist. Diese schützt das Gebäude wie ein Schneckenhaus nach Norden, das andererseits zum Süden hin vollkommen offen ist, um das Sonnenlicht hereinzulassen und das Haus auf ein weniger dicht besiedeltes Gebiet hin zu orientieren.

Carlo Scarpa fut chargé de ce projet par l'avocat Luigi Veritti, parent d'Angelo Masieri qui, comme Scarpa, s'intéressait à l'architecture de Frank Lloyd Wright. Le terrain à bâtir recommandé par Scarpa se trouvait dans une région peu construite. Le client avait toutefois choisi un terrain long et étroit à la périphérie d'Udine. En gros deux problèmes se posèrent: premièrement, la forme allongée du terrain et deuxièmement, le caractère amorphe de la zone résidentielle – qui n'était plus nature et pas encore ville, avec une urbanisation sauvage –, paysage typique à la périphérie des villes actuelles.

Quand les conditions spatiales étaient étroites, Scarpa avait tendance à réaliser des constructions arrondies. «On peut fort bien avoir des passages étroits quand l'espace s'élargit de nouveau, et on y parvient en courbant les murs», disait Scarpa. Pour éviter que le plan aux arrangements orthogonaux ne répète la rectangularité sévère du terrain, Scarpa imagina un plan fait de deux cercles. Mais pendant la phase centrale du travail, le second cercle perdit de plus en plus d'importance et se métamorphosa en jardin d'hiver; le client souhaitait un bâtiment plus compact qui s'étend donc maintenant sur deux étages. Mais ces propositions, qui essayaient de coordonner les idées de l'architecte et les désirs du client, ne furent pas réalisées. Les éléments de construction jusque-là différents se superposent désormais et définissent un corps unique entouré par un mur en forme de demi-cylindre. Celui-ci protège le bâtiment vers le nord comme une coquille d'escargot qui est d'ailleurs entièrement ouverte vers le sud pour faire entrer le soleil et orienter la maison vers une zone moins bâtie.

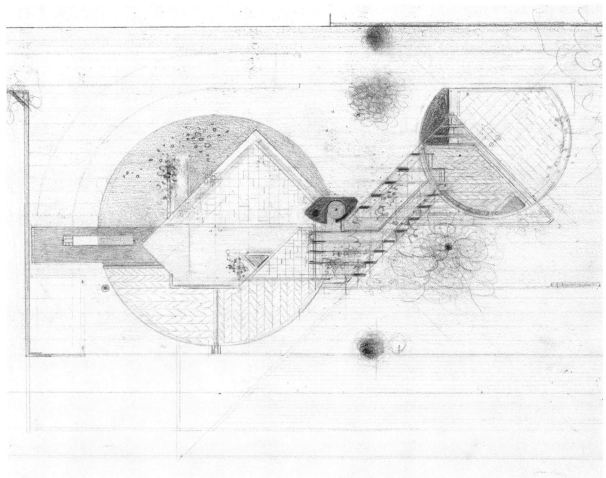

CASTELVECCHIO MUSEUM

Verona, 1956–1964
In collaboration with: C. Maschietto, A. Rudi

In connection with the 1957 exhibition »Da Altichiero a Pisanello«, Scarpa was commissioned only to restore the living quarters of the former citadel of Verona. But he did not limit himself to repairs; he tried by individual exposures and a little judicious demolition to reveal the different historical strata of the structural complex. He wanted to disentangle the periods of building, to show the building itself as a great museum in itself and, by his repairs, to reveal the phases of enlargement and structural alteration. Scarpa was more interested in historical transparency than in the theory of restoration; he wanted to make history come alive by a well-ordered juxtaposition of the fragments.

The walls are Roman in origin. During the period of the city states, Castelvecchio was split in two by its second line of fortifications. In the third construction phase, under the Scaligers between 1354 and 1356, the fortified walls were extended along with the building of the castle and the bridge over the Adige. The castle, the seat of the nobility, protected them from popular insurrection; it never served the people of Verona as a refuge but was open to the allied territories to the north. The bridge was the nobility's escape route. The Scaligers' castle was split by the city walls, with the living quarters to the west and the defences to the east. Between the two parts were the Torre del Mastio, controlling the bridge and river, and two trenches: the second, uncovered by Scarpa, follows the city walls. Even under the rule of Venice, the city fulfilled its military task. Later the French fortified the north side also and built an L-shaped barracks, which now contains most of the collections.

The last stage was the 1923 restoration, when the architect Forlati and the museum curator Avena provided the castle with a historical »mask« to convert it into a museum. In other words they plastered the barrack-front with a collage of Gothic »finds« and converted the whole fortified section into a palazzo. This was the state in which Scarpa found it.

Im Zusammenhang mit der Ausstellung »Da Altichiero a Pisanello« von 1957 war an Scarpa eigentlich nur der Auftrag ergangen, den Wohntrakt der ehemaligen Zitadelle von Verona zu restaurieren. Scarpa beschränkte sich jedoch nicht auf die Instandsetzungsarbeiten, sondern versuchte mit einzelnen Freilegungen und mit dem einen oder anderen gezielten Abriß die verschiedenen historischen Schichten des Gebäudekomplexes sichtbar zu machen. Es ging ihm darum, die Verflechtungen der Bauperioden zu entwirren, um das Gebäude selbst als großartiges Museumsstück zu thematisieren und die Phasen der baulichen Erweiterungen und strukturellen Veränderungen durch die Restaurierungsarbeit deutlich werden zu lassen. Mehr als die Theorie des Restaurierens interessierte Scarpa die »historische Klarheit«, das heißt, die Geschichte durch das geordnete Nebeneinander ihrer Fragmente sichtbar zu machen.

Die Mauern sind römischen Ursprungs. Zur Zeit der Stadtstaaten war Castelvecchio durch eine zweite Befestigungsanlage geteilt worden. In der dritten Bauphase, unter den Scaligern, wurden die Befestigungsmauern zwischen 1354 und 1356 – zusammen mit dem Bau des Kastells und der Brücke über die Etsch – erweitert. Die Burg war Sitz der Adelsherren und Bollwerk gegen die Aufstände der Stadtbevölkerung. Sie diente nie den Veronesern als Zuflucht, sondern war nach Norden, zu den verbündeten Territorien hin, offen: Die Brücke war der Fluchtweg für die Burgherren. Der Adelssitz der Scaliger war durch die Stadtmauern zweigeteilt: Der Wohntrakt lag im Westen, der Wehrbereich im Osten; zwischen den beiden Teilen befinden sich der Torre del Mastio, zur Kontrolle von Brücke und Fluß, und zwei Gräben, von denen der zweite – von Scarpa freigelegt – entlang der Stadtmauer verläuft. Auch unter der Herrschaft von Venedig erfüllte die Zitadelle weiterhin ihre militärische Aufgabe. Später befestigten die Franzosen auch die nördliche Seite und bauten dort eine L-förmige Kaserne, in der sich jetzt der größte Teil der ausgestellten Sammlung befindet.

Letzte Etappe war die Restaurierung von 1923: Der Architekt Forlati und der Museumsdirektor Avena versahen die Burg, um sie in ein Museum umzuwandeln, mit einer historischen »Maske«, das heißt, sie ersetzten die Fassade der Kaserne durch eine Collage von gotischen Einzelfundstücken und verwandelten den ganzen Wehrbereich in einen mittelalterlichen Palazzo. In diesem Zustand fand Scarpa das Gebäude vor.

Dans le cadre de l'exposition «Da Altichiero a Pisanello» de 1957, Scarpa avait à vrai dire seulement été chargé de restaurer l'aile d'habitation de l'ancienne citadelle de Vérone. Il ne se limita toutefois pas aux travaux de réparation, mais pratiqua des déblayages isolés et des démolitions ciblées afin de montrer les différentes couches historiques de l'ensemble des bâtiments. Il lui importait de débrouiller les interpénétrations des périodes de construction afin de prendre pour objet le bâtiment lui-même comme musée grandiose et de mettre en lumière les phases de l'agrandissement de la construction et de la modification structurelle par le travail de restauration. Scarpa s'intéressait davantage à la théorie de la restauration qu'à la «clarté historique», à savoir expliquer l'histoire par la juxtaposition ordonnée des fragments.

Les murs sont d'origine romaine. A l'époque des villes-Etats, Castelvecchio était divisé en deux par une partie des secondes fortifications. Au cours de la troisième phase de construction, sous les Scaliger, les murs des fortifications furent étendus entre 1354 et 1356 avec la construction du fort romain et du pont sur l'Adige. Le fort était à la fois le siège de l'aristocratie et un bastion contre les soulèvements de la population urbaine; il ne servit jamais de refuge aux Véronais, mais était ouvert vers le nord, vers les territoires alliés: le pont était le chemin des châtelains en fuite. Le siège de la noblesse des Scaliger était partagé en deux par les remparts: l'aile d'habitation à l'ouest, le secteur militaire à l'est; entre les deux parties se trouvent la Torre del Mastio, qui contrôle le pont et le fleuve, et deux fossés, dont le second – dégagé par Scarpa – longe les remparts. Sous la domination de Venise, la citadelle continua également à remplir sa fonction militaire. Par la suite, les Français fortifièrent aussi le côté nord et y construisirent une caserne en forme de L, dans laquelle se trouve actuellement la majeure partie de la collection exposée.

La dernière étape fut la restauration de 1923: l'architecte Forlati et le directeur du musée Avena nantirent alors le fort d'un «masque» historique pour le transformer en musée, c'est-à-dire qu'ils remplacèrent la façade de la caserne par un collage de pièces gothiques individuelles et métamorphosèrent l'ensemble du secteur militaire en palazzo. C'est dans cet état que Scarpa trouva le bâtiment.

Design for the inner courtyard (above); north façade with the central loggia overlooking the courtyard (below and right page)

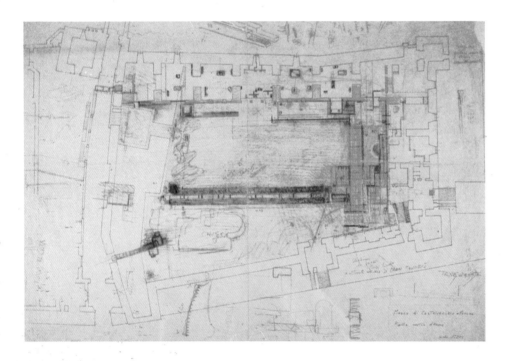

Some knowledge of this historical development is necessary to understand Scarpa's work, to show how he used architecture to explain what has just been said. »Castelvecchio was all deception«, said Scarpa in 1978, with regard to the elevation which leads to the courtyard. »I decided to introduce some vertical elements to break up the symmetry as the Gothic demanded; Gothic, especially in its Venetian form, is not very symmetrical«. The entrance first had to be moved away from the centre. Scarpa wanted the façade to stand out as a backcloth, and this he achieved mainly by the fenestration. The windows are not related to the façade but to the internal walls. Projecting elements such as the wall at the entrance or the floor areas were extended from inside to outside to help put across this inner wall as a part of the courtyard. Castelvecchio shows more than anywhere else how Scarpa's architecture is based on juxtaposition. There is a dialogue between different materials from different historical eras, placed close together yet apart. Hence the breaks: the newly-laid floors, like carpets, stop some distance short of the walls, while the walls in turn stop short of the ceilings. Scarpa completely demolished a narrow strip of façade so as to expose the different hidden layers of the building. He made this break a place of synthesis for the whole structure and emphasized it by the statue of Cangrande della Scala. The statue stands where the historical interconnections are clearest, high up on a stone slab set askew on a concrete base. Near the entrance, almost hidden by a concrete crosswall, a small shrine stands out from the façade, a little chapel displaying precious Lombard »finds«. Outside it is clad with small Prun stone slabs of different colour intensity, and alternately rough and smooth. Inside it is painted with bottle-green lime wash; the brick floor is edged with metal frames.

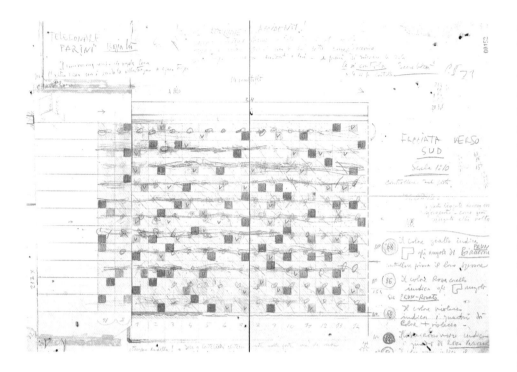

Man muß diese geschichtliche Entwicklung in etwa kennen, um Scarpas architektonischen Eingriff zu verstehen. Nur so kann man sehen, wie er die Architektur einsetzte, um etwas zu erklären, was hier mit Worten dargestellt wurde. »In Castelvecchio war alles Täuschung«, sagte Scarpa 1978 im Hinblick auf die Fassade, die zum Innenhof führt. »Ich beschloß, einige vertikal wirkende Elemente einzufügen, um die Symmetrie aufzubrechen, das verlangte das Gotische; und die Gotik, zumal die venezianische, ist nicht sehr symmetrisch.« Vor allem wurde der Eingang aus der Mitte versetzt. Scarpa wollte, daß die Fassade sich deutlich als eine Kulisse zu erkennen gibt, was er insbesondere mit der Gestaltung der Fenster erreichte. Sie beziehen sich ganz offensichtlich nicht auf die Fassade, sondern auf die innenliegende Wandfläche. Die Vermittlung dieser inneren Wandfläche zum Hof übernehmen vorspringende Elemente, wie die Mauer am Eingang oder die in den Außenbereich hinein verlängerten Bodenflächen. Mehr als anderswo wird hier in Castelvecchio erkennbar, wie sehr Scarpas Architektur auf dem Prinzip des Nebeneinanderstellens beruht. Es sind sowohl die unterschiedlichen Materialien als auch die verschiedenen Geschichtsepochen, die – nebeneinandergestellt und doch streng voneinander geschieden – miteinander in Dialog treten. Deshalb die Brüche: Die neu angelegten Böden halten wie Teppiche immer einen deutlichen Abstand zur Wand, die Mauern einen deutlichen Abstand zu den Decken.

Ein schmales Fassadenstück läßt Scarpa vollständig abreißen, um dadurch die verschiedenen verborgenen Schichten des Gebäudes aufzudecken. Diese Bruchstelle macht er zum Ort der Synthese des gesamten Werks und betont sie durch die Statue des Cangrande della Scala. Die Skulptur steht gerade dort, wo die historische Verflechtung am deutlichsten wird, hoch oben auf einer schräg auf einen Betonsockel gesetzten Steinplatte.

Nahe beim Eingang, fast versteckt hinter einer Quermauer aus Beton, ragt aus der Fassade ein kleiner Schrein hervor, eine Kapelle, in der wertvolle langobardische Fundstücke ausgestellt sind. Außen ist sie mit kleinen Prunsteinplatten von unterschiedlicher Farbintensität und von abwechselnd rauher und glatter Oberfläche verkleidet. Innen wurden die Mauern mit flaschengrünem Kalk glattgestrichen, den Boden bilden eisengefaßte Backsteinflächen.

Il faut connaître approximativement cette évolution historique pour comprendre l'intervention architectonique de Scarpa. C'est seulement de cette façon que l'on peut voir comment il utilisa l'architecture pour expliquer l'histoire d'une restauration. «A Castelvecchio, tout était tromperie», a dit Scarpa en 1978 en considération de la façade qui mène dans la cour intérieure: «J'ai décidé d'insérer quelques éléments verticaux pour casser la symétrie, le gothique l'exigeait; et le gothique, surtout le gothique vénitien, n'est pas très symétrique.» En premier lieu, l'entrée fut décalée par rapport au milieu. Scarpa voulait que la façade se fasse nettement reconnaître comme coulisse et y réussit en particulier avec la réalisation des fenêtres. Elles ne se réfèrent apparemment pas à la façade, mais à la surface murale intérieure. L'intervention de cette surface murale intérieure donnant sur la cour est reprise par des éléments faisant saillie, comme le mur à l'entrée ou les sols qui se prolongent à l'extérieur.

Plus qu'ailleurs, on voit à Castelvecchio combien l'architecture de Scarpa repose sur le principe de la juxtaposition. Divers matériaux et diverses époques historiques placés les uns à côté des autres, et pourtant toujours séparés les uns des autres, ont un dialogue. C'est la raison des cassures: pareils à des tapis, les sols nouvellement créés sont à une bonne distance du mur, les murs à une bonne distance des plafonds.

Scarpa fit entièrement démolir un étroit morceau de façade pour découvrir les diverses couches cachées du bâtiment. Il a fait de cette cassure le lieu de la synthèse de l'œuvre entière et l'a soulignée avec la statue du Cangrande della Scala. La statue se trouve justement à l'endroit où l'interpénétration historique est la plus nette, tout en haut, sur une dalle posée en diagonale sur un socle en béton. Près de l'entrée, presque caché derrière un mur transversal en béton, un petit sanctuaire forme une saillie sur la façade; il s'agit-là d'une petite chapelle dans laquelle sont exposés de précieux objets lombards. A l'extérieur, elle est revêtue de petits carreaux en pierre de Prun de diverses couleurs dont la surface est tour à tour lisse ou rugueuse. A l'intérieur, elle a été lissée avec de la chaux vert bouteille, tandis que le sol est formé par des dalles entourées de métal.

Design and execution of the Prun stone cladding of the »Sacello« (left page); entrance to the museum (below)

The Sculpture Gallery on the ground floor, with
works from the 12th to the 15th century

The fifth and final room of the Sculpture Gallery;
a »window« in the floor providing a glimpse of a newly
exposed section of the former castle moat (below);
»Crocefissione e Santi« in the fourth room of the
Gallery (right page)

The exhibition rooms date from Napoleonic times and are arranged in sequence. Scarpa used subdued materials alternating with selected episodes as a commentary to frame the exhibits. The plaster is based on slaked lime, more or less rough, depending on the coarseness of the sand added. The floor of rough-hewn concrete is edged with stone from Prun. The walls in the arched passages were clad with large rough slabs of pink Prun stone, familiar in the boundary walls of the old estates. An arched doorway with a grating of steel leads into the great courtyard where the Cangrande statue stands.

Die Ausstellungsräume stammen noch aus napoleonischer Zeit und sind als »enfilade«, als Raumfolge, angeordnet. Bei der Ausgestaltung verwendete Scarpa bewußt zurückhaltende Materialien, allerdings im Wechsel mit ausgesuchten Episoden, als kommentierenden Rahmen für die ausgestellten Werke. Der Verputz auf Löschkalkbasis ist mehr oder weniger rauh, je nach Körnung des Zuschlags. Die Bodenflächen aus behauenem Zement sind mit Prunstein gefaßt. Die Wände der Rundbogenpassagen wurden mit großen rauhen Platten aus rosafarbenem Prunstein verkleidet, wie man sie von den Grenzmauern der alten Gutshöfe kennt. Eine Bogentür mit einem Stahlgitter führt in den großen Innenhofbereich, wo die Statue des Cangrande steht.

Les salles d'exposition datent de l'époque napoléonienne et sont organisées comme une «enfilade». Pour la décoration, Scarpa a volontairement employé des matériaux discrets alternés avec des réalisations recherchées, de manière à avoir un cadre commentant les œuvres exposées. Le crépi à base de chaux éteinte est plus ou moins rugueux, selon le grain. Les sols en ciment taillé sont bordés de pierre de Prun. Les murs des passages avec arcs en plein-cintre ont été revêtus de grandes dalles rugueuses en pierre de Prun rose, comme celles des murs d'enceinte des anciennes fermes. Une porte en forme d'arc avec une grille métallique mène dans le grand espace intérieur où se trouve la statue de Cangrande.

View of the Cangrande space from the south
(below); view from the level of Cangrande bridge
(right page)

A maze of steps at various levels, after Pira-
nesi, leads to the western part of the courtyard
inside the city walls. This leads to the Torre
del Mastio and then to the living area, which
displays works by Veronese and Venetian
painters as well as some sculptures from the
early Middle Ages up till the fifteenth century.
It is possible to walk along the battlements so
as to end one's tour in the gallery containing
paintings from the fifteenth to the eighteenth
centuries.

Some of Scarpa's tricks in the art displays are
worth mentioning. Every exhibit had its own
specially designed plinth, suspension or support. In the process he designed complete
rooms with unusual combinations, using perspective to produce discoveries, aiming especially for the right light on each picture. He
placed some pictures on the type of easel
which he designed for the Correr museum so
as to allow the visitor to get close to the picture. Elsewhere a picture may only gradually
become visible or certain elements may be
specially emphasized by the lighting. Scarpa's
technique of »corner placing« is interesting:
when he hangs the picture between two steel
bars he shows the canvas as an art element on
its own.

For Scarpa museum architecture is therefore
not simply a way of housing art works, nor is it
a display machine: it is a critical tool that
makes art accessible and understandable.

Ein piranesisches Stufenlabyrinth auf verschiedenen Ebenen führt zum westlichen Innenhof.
Man gelangt von dort zum Torre del Mastio
und weiter zum Wohntrakt, in dem die Gemälde Veroneser und venezianischer Maler
sowie einige Skulpturen aus dem Mittelalter
bis zum 15. Jahrhundert untergebracht sind.
Von dort kehrt man zurück zur ehemaligen
Kaserne. Man kann auch den Weg entlang der
Zinnen wählen, um den Rundgang in der Galerie zu beenden, die Gemälde vom 15. bis
zum 18. Jahrhundert enthält.

Einige Kunstgriffe bei der Präsentation der
Ausstellungsstücke sind noch zu erwähnen.
Scarpa entwarf Sockel, Hängevorrichtungen
oder Stützkonstruktionen, immer direkt auf
das Exponat bezogen. Dabei gestaltete er ganze Räume, wagte ungewohnte Zusammenstel-
lungen, bediente sich der Wirkung der Per-
spektive, um dem Besucher Entdeckungen zu
ermöglichen, und sorgte insbesondere auch
für die »richtige« Ausrichtung der Bilder auf
das Licht. Teilweise plazierte er die Gemälde
auf Staffeleien – die gleichen, die er für das
Museo Correr entworfen hatte –, um so den

Besucher zu veranlassen, näher zu treten und dem Gemälde seine Aufmerksamkeit zu schenken. An anderer Stelle wird ein Bild erst allmählich sichtbar, oder bestimmte Elemente werden durch die Ausrichtung zum Licht besonders hervorgehoben. Interessant ist auch die Art und Weise, wie Carlo Scarpa die Plazierung im Winkel gestaltet: Wenn er das Gemälde zwischen zwei Stahlstangen aufhängt, um die Leinwand als eigenes Kunstelement zu zeigen.

Museumsarchitektur ist für Scarpa nicht einfach das Unterbringen von Kunstwerken; ein von ihm gestaltetes Gebäude ist keine Ausstellungsmaschine, sondern ein kritisches Instrument, das Kunstwerke wahrnehmbar und verstehbar macht.

Un labyrinthe piranésien en gradins sur différents niveaux mène à la cour intérieure de l'ouest. On arrive ensuite à la Torre del Mastio, puis à l'aile d'habitation où se trouvent des tableaux de peintres vénitiens et véronais ainsi que quelques sculptures du Moyen Age au XVe siècle. De là, on retourne à l'ancienne caserne. Il est également possible de marcher le long des créneaux pour terminer le tour dans la galerie qui abrite des tableaux du XVe au XVIIIe siècle.

Citons encore quelques interventions dans la présentation des pièces exposées. Scarpa a conçu des socles, des systèmes de suspension ou des constructions de soutien se rapportant toujours directement à l'objet exposé. Il a ainsi réalisé des salles entières, a osé des combinaisons inhabituelles, s'est servi de l'effet de la perspective, pour rendre possibles des découvertes, et s'est particulièrement intéressé à la «juste» orientation des toiles vers la lumière. Il a partiellement placé les tableaux sur des chevalets – ceux-là même qu'il avait conçus pour le Museo Correr – pour inciter le spectateur à s'approcher et à prêter son attention au tableau. Ailleurs, une toile ne devient visible que petit à petit, ou certains éléments sont particulièrement soulignés par l'orientation vers la lumière. Il est également intéressant de noter la manière dont Scarpa place les objets dans les coins: il suspend le tableau entre deux barres métalliques pour montrer la toile comme élément artistique autonome. L'architecture de musée n'est pas pour Scarpa seulement un lieu servant à caser les œuvres d'art, ni une machine à exposer. C'est un instrument critique qui rend les œuvres d'art perceptibles et compréhensibles.

Arrangement of paintings in the »Reggia«, the
residential part of the former fortress

»Madonna incoronata« in the third room of the
Sculpture Gallery (above); design and execution
of the support for the »Madonna con bambino«
in ivory (below and right page)

Following double page: »Paragoni« display
stands in the fourth room of the Upper Gallery
(left); new staircase in the »Reggia« (right)

OLIVETTI SHOWROOM

Venice, 1957–1958
In collaboration with: G. D'Agaro, C. Maschietto

Scarpa was commissioned to design the Olivetti showroom on the Piazza San Marco in Venice after he and Ludovico Quaroni were awarded the Olivetti Prize for Architecture in 1956. Adriano Olivetti was without doubt a most important personality for Italian culture, one of the last great patrons. It is no surprise, therefore, that he entrusted the refurbishing to Carlo Scarpa, who at the time in question was little known in Italy.

The task was difficult: to exploit a narrow, long and relatively dark space that first had to be put into some sort of order. This meant strengthening the structure and removing the old fittings in order to carry out the real architectural surgery, which transformed the space by means of a gradual modulation of the light, from the display windows in the arcade to the rear window overlooking the canal with its delicate lattice of costly teak and palisander filtering the reflections from the water. From every point, the room is seen as a whole. The upper level, reached by magnificent marble stairs, consists of long, low galleries lit by almond-shaped windows looking like eyes down on to the Piazza.

Den Auftrag, die Geschäftsräume der Firma Olivetti an der Piazza San Marco in Venedig einzurichten, erhielt Scarpa, nachdem er 1956 zusammen mit Ludovico Quaroni den Premio Olivetti für Architektur erhalten hatte. Adriano Olivetti war zweifellos eine für die italienische Kultur äußerst wichtige Persönlichkeit, einer der letzten »Mäzene«. Es überrascht daher nicht, daß er dem damals in Italien noch wenig bekannten Carlo Scarpa die Neueinrichtung anvertraute.

Die gegebenen Räumlichkeiten stellten ihn vor eine schwierige Aufgabe: Es galt, einen schmalen, langen und relativ dunklen Raum zu gestalten. Zunächst waren einige Vorarbeiten zu leisten: Die Baustruktur mußte gefestigt und die alte Ausstattung entfernt werden. Erst dann konnte ein architektonischer Eingriff vorgenommen werden, der den Raum durch eine schrittweise Modulation des Lichtes veränderte: von den großen Schaufenstern im Bogengang bis zum rückwärtigen Fenster, zum Kanal hin, dessen preziöses Gitter aus wertvollem Teak und Palisander die Lichtspiegelungen des Wassers filtert. Man erfaßt den Raum immer in seiner Gesamtheit. Die obere Ebene, zu der man über eine prächtige Marmortreppe gelangt, wird von langen, niedrigen Galerien gebildet. Diese erhalten ihr Licht wiederum durch mandelförmige Öffnungen, die wie Augen auf die Piazza blicken.

Scarpa fut chargé d'aménager les locaux commerciaux de la firme Olivetti, sur la place Saint-Marc à Venise, après avoir reçu le Premio Olivetti d'architecture avec Ludovico Quaroni. Adriano Olivetti était sans aucun doute une personnalité extrêmement importante pour la culture italienne, l'un des derniers «mécènes». Il n'est donc pas surprenant qu'il ait confié le réaménagement à Carlo Scarpa, alors peu connu en Italie.

Les lieux posaient un problème difficile: il s'agissait en effet d'aménager une pièce étroite, longue et relativement sombre. Il fallait tout d'abord mettre pas mal de choses en ordre, à savoir consolider la structure bâtie et faire disparaître l'ancien ameublement pour pouvoir pratiquer ensuite une intervention architectonique. Celle-ci modifia l'espace grâce à une modulation progressive de la lumière, depuis les grandes vitrines sous les arcades avec vue sur la Piazza jusqu'aux fenêtres donnant sur le canal, dont les précieuses grilles en bois de teck et en palissandre filtrent le miroitement de l'eau. On saisit ainsi toujours l'espace dans sa totalité. Le niveau supérieur, auquel on accède par un splendide escalier en marbre, est constitué par de longues galeries basses qui reçoivent à leur tour de la lumière par des ouvertures en amande regardant la Piazza, comme des yeux.

Side entrance (below); shop-windows and main
entrance to the Piazza San Marco (right page)

The passage through the room is eventful yet clearly outlined. Even the entrance from the side heralds the lack of symmetry in the inner passage. The little entrance hall is dominated by Alberto Viani's sculpture, which is reflected in a shallow black marble pool. Further back is the stair with its riserless stone steps hovering like a neoplastic deconstruction of Michelangelo's Laurenziana ramp, relaxing the stiff rectangular space by its cascade of steps. This staircase of Aurisina marble leads up to the mezzanine level, whose parapet both links the spatial elements and sets them off against each other. The gallery side is veneered with African teak; the lower side overlooking the floor below has a polished Venetian hard-plaster surface.

Massive pilasters are a frequent motif in Scarpa's work. Stone slabs, ending unmistakably below the level of the ceiling, advertise both their function as mere cladding and the montage quality of the ensemble. The artificial light throughout comes from vertical strips of satin glass hiding fluorescent tubes. Individual lighting is provided by small ebony lamps on stainless steel standards.

The rhythmically placed display windows in the arcade are flush with the façade, without ledge, overhang or other shadowing. The thick glass is held in a brass frame. All screwed connections are sealed while the edges are bevelled at 45 degrees in order to soften the harshness of the rectangular frame. Scarpa designed elegant, miniature wooden trays hung from the ceiling so that the products might be displayed without obstructing the lighting or the view into the room.

The floor, 31 centimetres above the Piazza, is remarkable enough to have been copied often. Its decorative pattern of Murano glass is composed of four different colours, each in four different sizes. The pattern is quite deliberate although it is intentionally irregular, based on pictorial motifs by Paul Klee. It gives the feeling of a moving surface, as if it were permanently under water.

Der Durchgang durch den Raum ist reich an Ereignissen und dennoch klar konturiert. Schon der seitlich angelegte Eingang kündigt die Asymmetrie des Weges im Innern an. Die kleine Eingangshalle wird beherrscht von einer goldglänzenden Skulptur von Alberto Viani, die sich in einem flachen Wasserbecken aus schwarzem Marmor spiegelt. Weiter hinten dann die Treppe mit ihren schwebenden Steinplatten, die eine neoplastische Dekonstruktion der Laurenziana-Rampe von Michelangelo darstellt und die den prismatischen Raum mit ihrer informellen, nach unten drängenden Kaskade von Stufen auflockert. Diese Treppe aus Aurisina-Marmor führt hinauf zum Zwischenstockwerk, dessen Brüstung die verschiedenen Raummomente sowohl miteinander verbindet als auch voneinander abhebt. Zur Galerie hin ist sie mit afrikanischem Teakholz furniert, zur unteren Etage hin zeigt sie polierten venezianischen Stuck.

Wuchtige Pilaster stellen ein häufig wiederkehrendes Kompositionselement bei Scarpa dar. Steinplatten, die deutlich unter dem Deckenniveau enden, demonstrieren dabei ihre bloße Funktion als Verkleidung und den Montagecharakter. Die allgemeine künstliche Beleuchtung leisten vertikale Bänder aus satiniertem Glas, hinter denen Leuchtstoffröhren installiert sind. Für die Einzelbeleuchtung sorgen kleine Lampen aus Ebenholz an Stangen aus Edelstahl.

Die durch den Bogengang rhythmisch gegliederten Schaufenster sind direkt an der Fassadenvorderkante eingelassen, ohne Sims, Vor- oder Rücksprung. Das dicke Glas wird von einem Messingrahmen gehalten. Alle Verschraubungen sind verplombt, die Ecken des Rahmens um 45 Grad abgeschrägt, um die Strenge des Rechtecks zu mildern. Zur Präsentation der Produkte entwarf Scarpa elegante, von der Decke abgehängte Holztischchen, die den Blick in den Raum nicht verstellen. Bemerkenswert ist im übrigen auch der Fußboden, der häufig nachgeahmt wurde. Er ist gegenüber der Piazza um 31 Zentimeter erhöht, und sein Muster aus Muranoglas setzt sich aus vier verschiedenen Farben und vier verschiedenen Größen je Farbe zusammen. Das Muster verläuft entlang genau vorgegebener Linien, ist jedoch von gewollter Unregelmäßigkeit und folgt Bildmotiven von Paul Klee. Damit wird der Effekt einer bewegten Oberfläche erzeugt, als ob der Boden immer unter Hochwasser stünde.

Le passage à travers la pièce est riche en événements et pourtant clairement esquissé. L'entrée latérale annonce déjà l'asymétrie du chemin à l'intérieur. Le petit hall d'entrée est dominé par une sculpture dorée d'Alberto Viani qui se reflète dans un bassin plat en marbre noir. Plus loin, vers le fond, se trouve l'escalier en dalles suspendues, qui représente une «déconstruction» néo-plastique de la rampe de la bibliothèque Laurentienne bâtie par Michel-Ange et aère l'espace prismatique avec sa cascade informelle de marches se pressant vers le bas. Cet escalier en marbre d'Aurisina mène à l'entresol, dont la balustrade relie les différents éléments de la pièce tout en les faisant ressortir. Vers la galerie, il est plaqué avec du bois de teck africain, vers l'étage inférieur, il est en stuc vénitien poli.

Les lourds pilastres représentent un élément structurel qui revient fréquemment chez Scarpa. Les dalles, qui se terminent nettement sous le niveau du plafond, démontrent leur simple fonction de revêtement et leur caractère de montage. L'éclairage artificiel général est réalisé par des bandes verticales en verre dépoli, derrière lesquelles sont montés des tubes fluorescents. De petites lampes en bois d'ébène fixées sur des barres en acier pourvoient à la lumière individuelle.

Les vitrines rythmiquement divisées par les arcades sont directement encastrées dans l'arête avant de la façade, sans rebord, ni saillie, ni nuances. Le verre épais est retenu par un cadre en laiton. Tous les raccords sont plombés, les coins du cadre sont taillés en biseau à 45 degrés, afin d'atténuer la sévérité du rectangle. Pour présenter les produits, Scarpa a conçu d'élégantes petites tables accrochées au plafond qui n'entravent pas la vue dans la pièce.

On remarquera en outre le sol, qui a souvent été imité. Il est surélevé de 31 centimètres par rapport à la Piazza, et son motif en verre de Murano est composé de quatre couleurs distinctes et de quatre dimensions différentes pour chaque couleur. L'arrangement longe des lignes données, tout en étant d'une irrégularité voulue, et suit des motifs picturaux de Paul Klee. Ceci produit un effet de surface agitée, comme si le sol était constamment inondé.

FONDAZIONE QUERINI-STAMPALIA

Venice, 1961–1963
In collaboration with: C. Maschietto

Giuseppe Mazzariol, Carlo Scarpa's friend and colleague at the Architectural Faculty of Venice, where Mazzariol lectured on architectural history, was Director of the Querini-Stampalia Foundation in the early sixties. When the decision to restore this sixteenth-century Venetian palace was taken, Mazzariol asked Scarpa to remodel both the ground floor, unusable because of periodic flooding, and the courtyard. The building houses exhibition rooms and the foundation's library and had been disfigured by a nineteenth-century reconstruction. The plan was to draw up a thoughtful design for the restoration of the palace to its pristine state.
As elsewhere, Scarpa's architectural surgery was executed with great sensitivity towards the natural and cultural context. For him, the water was not a problem but an inspiration. Instead of denying entry to it, Scarpa allowed it to flow off more freely, and, by raising the floors in the rooms at risk, guaranteed their continued use. By choosing appropriate materials, he reduced water problems to a minimum.

Giuseppe Mazzariol, Scarpas Freund und Kollege an der Architekturfakultät von Venedig, wo dieser Architekturgeschichte lehrte, war Anfang der sechziger Jahre Direktor der Stiftung Querini-Stampalia. Als man sich zu Restaurierungsarbeiten entschloß, beauftragte Mazzariol Scarpa mit der Umgestaltung sowohl des Erdgeschosses, das durch die periodisch auftretenden Hochwasser unbenutzbar geworden war, als auch des Innenhofes des venezianischen Palazzo aus dem 16. Jahrhundert. Dieser beherbergt Ausstellungsräume sowie die Bibliothek der Stiftung. Im übrigen hatte ein früherer, im 19. Jahrhundert erfolgter Umbau die ursprüngliche Räumlichkeit völlig entstellt, die nun mit einem kritischen Entwurf wiederhergestellt werden sollte.
Wie in anderen Fällen zeigt sich auch hier, daß Scarpa bei seinem architektonischen Eingriff mit großer Sensibilität auf den jeweils vorgegebenen Kontext – sowohl den kulturellen als auch den natürlichen – einging. So war das Wasser für Scarpa kein Problem, sondern Anlaß und Quelle der Inspiration. Statt ihm den Zugang zum Gebäude zu verwehren,

ging es Scarpa vielmehr darum, es ungehinderter abfließen zu lassen und durch eine Anhebung der Böden in den gefährdeten Räumen zugleich deren Nutzung sicherzustellen. Mit der Wahl geeigneter Materialien reduzierte er die durch das Wasser verursachten Unannehmlichkeiten auf ein Minimum.

Guiseppe Mazzariol, ami et collègue de Carlo Scarpa à la faculté d'architecture de Venise, où celui-ci enseignait l'histoire de l'architecture, était directeur de la fondation Querini-Stampalia au début des années soixante. Lorsqu'il fut décidé d'effectuer des travaux de restauration, Mazzariol chargea Scarpa de transformer le rez-de-chaussée, qui était devenu inutilisable à cause des inondations périodiques et la cour intérieure du Palazzo vénitien du XVIe siècle. Celui-ci abrite des salles d'exposition ainsi que la bibliothèque de la fondation. Une transformation antérieure effectuée au XIXe siècle avait au reste complètement défiguré les locaux originaux qui devaient être restaurés à l'aide d'un projet critique.
Comme dans d'autres cas, on voit, ici aussi, que dans son intervention architectonique Scarpa est entré avec une grande sensibilité dans le contexte donné – aussi bien culturel que naturel. Pour Scarpa, l'eau n'était pas un problème, mais un motif et une source d'inspiration. Au lieu de lui refuser l'accès au bâtiment, Scarpa préféra la laisser couler librement et garantir en même temps l'utilisation des pièces menacées en élevant le niveau du sol. En choisissant des matériaux appropriés, il parvint à réduire à un minimum les désagréments causés par l'eau.

The water now enters through a grating on the canal side of the ground floor, and flows through a small channel along the walls in such a way as not to prevent people from freely walking round the rooms. Thus the path becomes a catwalk, and the one-time obstacle became the motif of the design.

Das Wasser tritt nun an der dem Kanal zugewandten Seite des Erdgeschosses durch ein Gitter in das Gebäude ein und fließt weiter in einen kleinen Kanal, der so entlang der Wände angelegt wurde, daß er das Umhergehen in den Räumen nicht behindert. Damit wird der Weg zum Laufsteg, und das, was zuvor Hindernis war, wird Thema des Entwurfs.

Désormais, l'eau entre dans le bâtiment à travers une grille du côté du rez-de-chaussée qui est tourné vers le canal et poursuit son chemin dans un petit canal aménagé le long des murs, de sorte qu'il est possible de déambuler dans les pièces sans être gêné. Le chemin devient une passerelle, et ce qui était auparavant un obstacle devient ainsi le thème du projet.

»Causeway« in the flood-threatened ground floor

The entrance to the palazzo is over a bridge connecting it to the »campiello«, the little square beside the church of Santa Maria Formosa. The bridge is also typically Venetian. It is of steel, shaped like a drawn bow, and sits on blocks of Istrian stone – on one side directly at the frontage, on the other side at the street along the canal. The structure is built of two arches of sheet steel connected by massive square sections. The flat steel railing uprights are topped with a circular tube, together with a ship-style teak handrail. The railing itself is built up from three segments which, by their straightness, effectively serve to emphasize the arch shape of the little bridge. The stair treads are made of larch heartwood.

To the left of the bridge two identical gates close the two arches of the porch facing the canal. Each gate has two parts. The upper part is made of vertical round bars of a special brass alloy fixed into a iron frame. The lower part has iron sections of different thickness arranged in an oriental pattern.

After crossing the bridge and passing through the glass-sided porch, visitors find themselves standing on the marble floor of the entrance hall, a polychrome mosaic with motifs by Paul Klee already used by Scarpa in the Castelvecchio museum. The wall cladding consists of white plastered light masonry, placed slightly away from the wall to ensure ventilation and protect it from dampness. The ceilings are plastered with orange-red Venetian hard plaster. From the entrance hall, one passes a ceiling-high glass wall before climbing gently to the conference and exhibition hall. The need to conceal the new heating units involved Scarpa here in an elaborately sculptured cladding of Istrian stone.

Zum Eingang des Palazzo gelangt man über eine Brücke, die ihn mit dem »campiello«, dem kleinen Platz bei der Kirche Santa Maria Formosa, verbindet. Auch die Brücke ist ein typisch venezianisches Thema. Sie besteht aus einer Stahlkonstruktion, die die Form eines gespannten Bogens hat und auf Blöcken aus istrischem Stein ruht – auf der einen Seite wird sie so direkt an die Fassade herangeführt, auf der anderen setzt sie an der Kanalstraße am »campiello« an. Die tragende Konstruktion wird von zwei Bögen aus gekrümmten Stahlplatten gebildet, die durch massive Stege von quadratischem Zuschnitt miteinander verbunden sind. Die Geländerstützen aus Flacheisen tragen ein Rundrohr mit einem Handlauf aus Teakholz, der an Formen im Schiffsbau erinnert. Das Geländer besteht aus drei Segmenten, die mit ihrer geraden Führung die Bogenform der kleinen Brücke wirkungsvoll unterstreichen. Stufen und Trittfläche sind aus Lärchenkernholz.

Links von der Brücke verschließen zwei identische Gitter die beiden großen Rundbögen am Kanal. Jedes Gittertor besteht aus zwei Teilen: Der obere Teil wird von Rundstäben aus einer speziellen Messinglegierung gebildet, die vertikal in Eisenfassungen eingespannt sind; der untere Teil besteht aus Eisenprofilen von unterschiedlicher Stärke, die so angeordnet sind, daß sich ein an orientalische Motive erinnerndes Muster ergibt.

Hat man die Brücke und den Windfang aus Glas passiert, tritt man hinunter auf den marmornen Boden der Eingangshalle, ein polychromes Mosaik, das Motive von Paul Klee übernimmt, die Scarpa bereits im Museum Castelvecchio verwendet hatte. Die Wandverkleidung bilden weiß verputzte Paneele aus leichtem Mauerwerk, die mit einem gewissen Abstand zur Mauer verklammert sind, um deren Belüftung zu gewährleisten und sie vor Feuchtigkeit zu schützen. Die Decken sind mit orangerotem venezianischem Stuck überzogen. Von der Eingangshalle aus gelangt man, an einer deckenhohen Glaswand vorbei, zum höhergelegenen Konferenz- und Ausstellungsraum. Die notwendige Installation von Heizkörpern veranlaßte Scarpa hier zum Entwurf einer aufwendig ausgearbeiteten skulpturalen Verkleidung aus istrischem Stein.

On accède à l'entrée du palazzo par un pont qui le relie au «campiello», la petite place de l'église Santa Maria Formosa. Le pont est lui aussi un thème typiquement vénitien. Il est composé d'une construction en acier qui a la forme d'un arc tendu et repose sur des blocs de pierre d'Istrie – d'un côté, il est directement amené sur la façade, de l'autre, il est appliqué contre la rue du canal au bord du «campiello». La construction portante est formée de deux arcs en plaques d'acier courbes, reliés par des entretoises massives coupées au carré. Les supports du parapet en acier plat portent un tube avec une main courante en bois de teck qui rappelle les formes en usage dans la construction navale. Le garde-fou est constitué de trois segments qui soulignent efficacement la forme d'arc du petit pont avec leur barre conductrice droite. Les marches et le giron sont en bois de mélèze.

A gauche du pont, deux grilles identiques bouchent les deux grands arcs en plein-cintre au bord du canal. Chaque porte à claire-voie est constituée de deux parties: la partie supérieure est formée de bâtons ronds faits d'un alliage spécial de laiton qui sont tendus verticalement sur des châssis de fer; la partie inférieure est faite de fers profilés d'épaisseurs différentes qui sont arrangés de manière à former un dessin rappelant les motifs orientaux.

Une fois que l'on a passé le pont et le tambour en verre, on descend sur le sol de marbre du hall d'entrée, à savoir une mosaïque polychrome qui reprend des motifs de Paul Klee que Scarpa avait déjà utilisés dans le musée Castelvecchio. Le revêtement mural est constitué de panneaux crépis blancs en maçonnerie légère qui sont fixés avec des crampons à une certaine distance du mur, afin de garantir la ventilation de ce dernier et de le protéger contre l'humidité. Les plafonds sont enduits de stuc vénitien rouge-orangé. A partir du hall d'entrée, on passe devant une paroi de verre touchant le plafond pour accéder à la salle de conférences et d'expositions située plus haut. Comme il était nécessaire d'installer des radiateurs, Scarpa a conçu un luxueux revêtement sculptural en pierre d'Istrie.

In the large exhibition hall which extends to the courtyard, stone bands break up the exposed concrete of the plinths and floor. This floor is a modern interpretation of the traditional surfacing of stone and gravel used in the courtyards and »porteghi«, or colonnades, of a Venetian palazzo. Above the plinth the walls are clad with two broad strips of travertine marble from Rapolano, separated at eye level by a brass moulding. Fluorescent tubes protected by frosted glass are integrated flush with the stone cladding. The integration of a door leading to a small room reserved for those attending conferences is especially successful.

Im großen, bis zum Innenhof reichenden Ausstellungsraum gliedern Steinbänderungen die Fußboden- und Sockelflächen aus Waschbeton. Dieser Fußboden stellt eine moderne Interpretation der traditionellen Beläge aus Reihen von Stein und Kies dar, wie man sie in den Innenhöfen und den »porteghi«, den Säulengängen der venezianischen Palazzi, findet. Oberhalb des Wandsockels sind die Wände mit zwei breiten Bändern aus Rapolano-Travertin verkleidet, getrennt durch ein Messingprofil in Augenhöhe. Durch Milchglas abgeschirmte Leuchtstoffröhren sind vollkommen plan in die Steinverkleidung integriert. Besonders gelungen ist eine Tür in die Fläche eingebunden: Sie führt zu einem kleinen, Konferenzteilnehmern vorbehaltenen Zimmer.

Dans la grande salle d'exposition qui s'étend jusqu'à la cour intérieure, des bandes en pierre divisent les surfaces du sol et du socle en béton lavé. Ce sol représente une interprétation moderne des revêtements traditionnels constitués de rangées de pierre et de gravier comme on en trouve dans les cours intérieures et les «porteghi», colonnades des palazzi vénitiens. Au-dessus des lambris, les murs sont revêtus de deux larges bandes en travertin de Rapolano qui sont séparées par un profilé en laiton situé à hauteur des yeux. Des tubes fluorescents protégés par du verre dépoli sont également intégrés d'une manière parfaitement plane dans le revêtement en pierre. Une porte encastrée dans la surface est particulièrement réussie. Elle mène à une petite pièce réservée aux personnes participant à une conférence.

Details of the garden

The room opens on to the small, rectangular garden. Scarpa raised the garden level to create a more intimate relationship between indoors and out. One side of the garden is bounded by a concrete wall covered with a mosaic designed by Mario De Luigi, resembling that on the wall of the Brion family tomb.

The garden layout is Scarpa's interpretation of the traditional Venetian garden, in keeping with the regional character of the architecture. Water again has its chance. A small pool of violet marble from the Apulian Alps collects water dripping from a pipe and leads it through a maze of pools before it flows into a deep brook with water lilies. At the far end of a little pool where birds drink, the water flows over a little waterfall alongside the wall of an old well, now dry.

Scarpa's operation concludes with the design of the lift shaft and door and window locks, and the restoration of the stairs leading to the library on the first floor. On the landing is a particularly interesting lamp in a Brazilian rosewood frame, carried on a polygonally carved standard. Two frosted glass panes protect the bulbs.

Der Raum öffnet sich zu einem kleinen rechteckigen Garten hin, den Scarpa ebenfalls angehoben hat, um so eine engere Beziehung zwischen Innen und Außen herzustellen. Eine Seite dieses Gartens wird durch eine Zementmauer begrenzt, die mit einem von Mario De Luigi entworfenen Mosaik dekoriert ist und Ähnlichkeit mit der Mauer am Grabmal der Familie Brion hat.

Auch bei der Anlage des Gartens wird der Einfluß der venezianischen Tradition deutlich; jedoch hebt Scarpa dabei besonders den regionalen Charakter der Architektur hervor. Das Wasser hat erneut seinen Anteil am Spiel der Wege: Ein kleines Becken aus violettfarbenem Marmor aus den apuanischen Alpen sammelt das Wasser, das aus einer Röhre tropft, und läßt es in labyrinthischer Wegführung eine Reihe von Becken füllen. Schließlich ergießt es sich in einen tiefen Bach, in dem Seerosen wachsen. Am äußersten Ende des Beckens, wo Vögel ihren Durst löschen können, fließt das Wasser über einen sehr kleinen Wasserfall unmittelbar bei der Brüstung eines alten, inzwischen ausgetrockneten Brunnens ab. Scarpas architektonischer Eingriff findet seinen Abschluß in der Einrichtung des Aufzugsschachtes, dem Entwurf von Schließvorrichtungen für Türen und Fenster und der Erneuerung der Treppe, die zur Bibliothek im ersten Stock hinaufführt. Dort auf dem Treppenabsatz befindet sich eine besonders interessante Lampe, deren Rahmen aus brasilianischem Palisander gearbeitet ist und durch eine polygonal beschnittene Stange gehalten wird. Zwei Milchglasscheiben schirmen die Glühbirnen ab.

La pièce s'ouvre sur le jardin que Scarpa a également surélevé, afin de créer un rapport plus étroit entre l'intérieur et l'extérieur. Il est rectangulaire et de petites dimensions; l'un des côtés est fermé par un mur en ciment qui est décoré avec une mosaïque conçue par Mario De Luigi et ressemble au mur situé à côté du tombeau de la famille Brion.

Ce jardin représente également une adaptation du jardin vénitien traditionnel que Scarpa a interprété en soulignant le caractère régional de l'architecture. L'eau participe de nouveau au jeu des chemins: un petit bassin de marbre violet des Alpes apuaniennes rassemble l'eau qui s'égoutte d'un tuyau; après avoir suivi un tracé labyrinthique, elle remplit une série de bassins. Pour finir, elle s'écoule dans un ruisseau profond où poussent quelques nénuphars. A l'extrémité du petit bassin, où peuvent se désaltérer les oiseaux qui vivent dans le jardin, l'eau s'écoule au-dessus d'une toute petite cascade près de la balustrade d'une vieille fontaine entre-temps asséchée. L'intervention architectonique de Scarpa se termine par l'installation d'une cage d'ascenseur, le projet de mécanismes de fermeture pour les portes et les fenêtres et la rénovation de l'escalier menant à la bibliothèque, au premier étage. Là, sur le palier, se trouve une lampe particulièrement intéressante dont le cadre est fait en bois de palissandre brésilien et à travers laquelle est passée une baguette polygonale. Deux carreaux en verre dépoli protègent les ampoules électriques.

GAVINA SHOWROOM

Bologna, 1961–1963

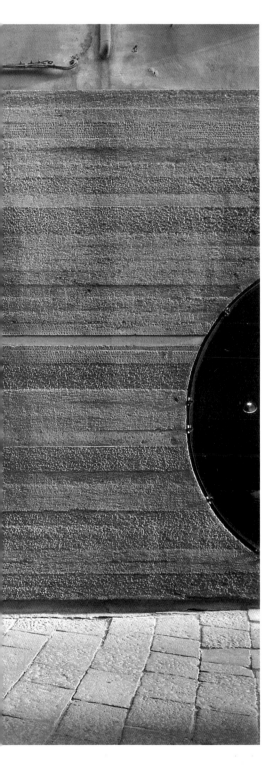

This shop, on the ground floor of a Bologna house, was previously an ironmonger's. Scarpa had to reshape an untidy space fragmented by load-bearing walls and unsuited to the client's display purposes.

Carlo Scarpa first set up a sort of shield, a large concrete slab chiselled in long strips and rhythmically structured by gilded stripes and by three openings, a double ring, a single ring, and the entrance in the middle. The glass of the display windows, flush with the front of the building, is held by bronze and cast-iron clamps.

Scarpa was always meticulous about thresholds. The theme of crossing over from one place to another was for him an inexhaustible source of invention. One can only speak of architecture when there is a clearly delimited area, a boundary between two units; that is what makes an awareness of transition, of passage, so important.

Scarpa here planned a small anteroom closed by a modestly dimensioned but elegant lattice door. It separates the inside from the outside and invites people to come in, but does not shut off the interior from the outside world. Built like a tool rack, it has steel sections carrying walnut wood battens. After passing through the little anteroom one passes by a revolving door into the shop. This door, built of Japanese fir, padauk wood and glass, allows the shop area to be seen before it is entered.

Das Geschäft befindet sich im Erdgeschoß eines Bologneser Wohnhauses, das zuvor eine Eisenwarenhandlung genutzt hatte. Scarpa sollte diesen unstrukturierten Raum neu gestalten, der durch die tragenden Wände zerstückelt und für die Ausstellungszwecke, die von den Auftraggebern gewünscht wurden, ungeeignet war.

Zunächst setzte Scarpa der ursprünglichen Fassade eine Art Schild vor, eine große Zementscheibe, streifenweise mit dem Meißel bearbeitet und rhythmisch gegliedert durch vergoldete Bänder sowie durch drei Öffnungen: ein Doppelkreis, eine einzelne Kreisöffnung und in der Mitte der Eingang. Die Schaufenster, deren Scheiben unmittelbar an der Fassadenkante anschließen, werden durch Bronze- und Gußeisenspangen gehalten.

Scarpa widmete den Schwellen immer besondere Aufmerksamkeit: Das Thema des Übergangs von einem Ort zum anderen, des Überschreitens, des Überquerens, war für ihn eine unerschöpfliche Quelle der Erfindung. Man kann erst dann von Architektur sprechen,

wenn es einen deutlich abgrenzbaren Bereich gibt, eine Grenzlinie, die zwei Einheiten trennt; deshalb ist das Bewußtsein des Überschreitens so wichtig.

In diesem Fall plante Scarpa einen kleinen Vorraum, der von einer bescheiden dimensionierten, aber eleganten Gittertür verschlossen wird. Sie trennt Innen und Außen, lädt zum Eintreten ein, aber schließt das Innen nicht gegen das Außen ab. Gearbeitet ist sie aus Eisenprofilen, in die, wie bei einem Geräteständer, Nußbaumstäbe eingesetzt sind. Wenn man dann einen kleinen Wandelgang passiert hat, gelangt man durch eine Drehtür ins Innere des Geschäfts. Diese Drehtür aus japanischer Tanne, Paduk und Kristallglas erlaubt, die Räume des Geschäfts schon vom Wandelgang aus zu überblicken.

Le magasin se trouve au rez-de-chaussée d'une maison d'habitation bolognaise qui abritait autrefois une quincaillerie. Scarpa devait réaménager cette pièce non structurée qui était morcelée par les murs porteurs et n'était pas adaptée aux expositions souhaitées par les clients.

Scarpa plaça d'abord une sorte de «bouclier» devant la façade existante, un grand disque en ciment en partie travaillé au burin et rythmiquement divisé par des bandes dorées et trois ouvertures: un double cercle, une ouverture circulaire individuelle et, au milieu, l'entrée. Les vitrines, dont les vitres sont directement posées sur l'arête de la façade, sont maintenues par des agrafes en bronze et en fonte.

Scarpa a toujours accordé une attention particulière aux seuils: le thème du passage d'un lieu à un autre, du franchissement, de la traversée était pour lui une inépuisable source d'invention. On peut seulement parler d'architecture quand il y a un domaine nettement délimitable, une limite qui sépare deux unités; c'est pour cela que la conscience du franchissement est si importante.

Dans ce cas, Scarpa conçut une petite antichambre fermée par une porte à claire-voie de dimensions modestes, mais élégante. Celle-ci sépare l'intérieur et l'extérieur, invite à entrer, mais n'isole pas l'intérieur de l'extérieur. Elle est travaillée avec des fers profilés dans lesquels sont passées des baguettes en noyer, comme pour les porte-outils.

Après avoir traversé un petit couloir, on parvient à l'intérieur du magasin en passant par une porte tournante. Cette porte tournante en sapin japonais, padouk et cristal, permet de voir les pièces du magasin depuis le couloir.

Service door (below); view towards the office side
with the »Doge« table designed by Carlo Scarpa
(right page)·

Scarpa exploited the vertical structural elements in the display rooms and, by exaggerating their size, converted them into plastic, coloured features of the spatial composition. Their materials include rough plaster, wood, black laminate, cobalt blue or brilliant white stucco with a silver coating. The brown synthetic flooring is separated from the wall by a stone gutter. The walls were limewashed. Instead of reducing the structural parts to a visual minimum, Scarpa exaggerated them. They almost lose their structural purpose and become more important as pure architecture.

In den Ausstellungsräumen nutzte Scarpa die vertikalen Strukturelemente, steigerte sie in ihren Dimensionen und machte sie zu plastischen, chromatischen Protagonisten der Raumkomposition. Als Materialien wurden rauher Putz, kobaltblauer oder glänzend kalkweißer Stuck mit Silberüberzug, Holz, schwarzes Laminat etc. verwendet. Der Fußboden besteht aus braunem Kunststoff und ist von den Wänden durch ein umlaufendes Rinnenprofil aus Stein abgesetzt. Die Wände wurden mit Kalk glattgestrichen. Statt die dominanten tragenden Elemente des Raumes also in ihrer Erscheinung auf ein zulässiges Minimum zu reduzieren, steigerte Scarpa vielmehr ihre Wirkung. So verlieren sie jeden Hinweis auf ihre tektonische Funktion und finden in der architektonischen Gestaltung ihre primäre Motivation.

Dans les salles d'exposition, Scarpa a utilisé des éléments structurels verticaux, les a renforcés dans leurs dimensions et en a fait les protagonistes plastiques et chromatiques de la composition spatiale. Les matériaux employés sont un crépi rugueux, du stuc bleu de cobalt ou blanc brillant avec un revêtement argenté, du bois, de l'aggloméré noir, etc. Le sol en plastique brun est séparé du mur par un profil en pierre en forme de gouttière. Les murs ont été badigeonnés à la chaux. Au lieu de réduire à un minimum admissible les éléments porteurs de la pièce dans leur apparence, Scarpa a donc au contraire intensifié leur effet. Ils perdent ainsi toute référence à leur fonction tectonique et trouvent dans l'architecture pure leur motivation primaire.

Details of the former Gavina showroom, now
Simon showroom

CASA CASSINA

Ronco di Carimate, Como, 1963–1964

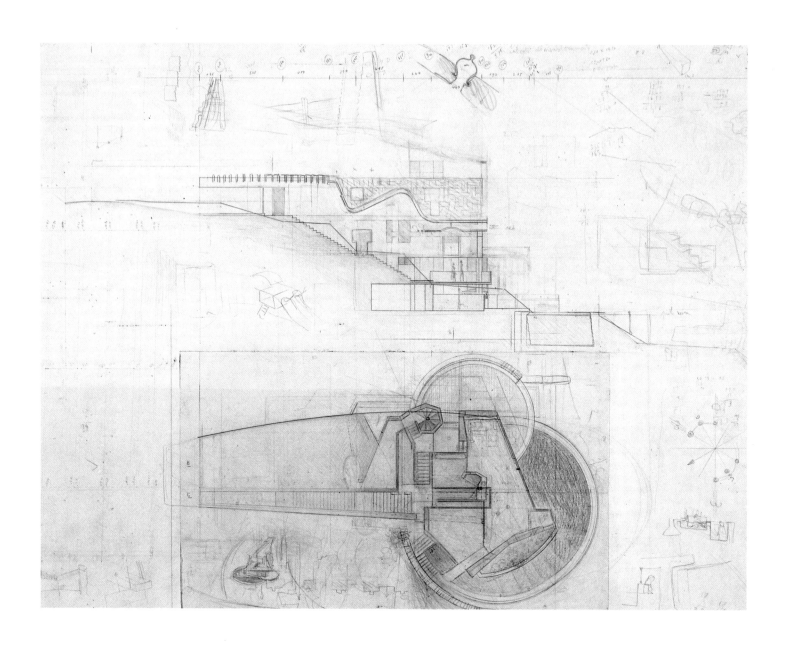

The Cassina house was a most unusual project in Scarpa's œuvre. The site was steep, and the building had to occupy as little space as possible. Scarpa sketched out several possible solutions, using terracing of the ground as a start for further design, and dug the rooms into the slope as far as was practicable. The rooms were at different levels along a curved wall, the line of which dominated the long building. The composition is rich with suggestive stimuli which reappear in the Ottolenghi house. A polygon drawn around a pool seems to anticipate several recent deconstructivist experiments, even allowing that Scarpa had no trangressive intention whatsoever.
A further design cut deep terraces into the slope for the living quarters. The whole ensemble was now rhythmically structured by small walls flanking the vertical structures which formed the bedrooms.
The client, one of the best-known patrons of Italian furniture design, found that Scarpa had not kept to agreed deadlines, and gave him an ultimatum. When Scarpa did not respond, the client cancelled the contract and gave the job to the architect Vico Magistretti, who built the house to a new design.

Das Haus Cassina ist in Scarpas Gesamtwerk ein recht ungewöhnliches Projekt. Das Gebäude sollte auf einem stark abfallenden Grundstück stehen und möglichst wenig Platz beanspruchen. Scarpa konzipierte verschiedene Lösungen, verwendete Terrassierungen als Ausgangspunkt für die weitere Entwurfsarbeit und baute die Räume so weit wie möglich in den Hang hinein. Die Zimmer waren auf unterschiedlichen Niveaus entlang einer gekurvten Mauer angeordnet, deren Linie den langen Baukörper beherrscht. Die Komposition ist reich an suggestiven Reizen, die man auch im Haus Ottolenghi findet. Die polygonale Anordnung der Linien, die ein Wasserbecken umschreiben, nimmt bereits einige neuere dekonstruktivistische Experimente vorweg, auch wenn bei Scarpa jede polemische Intention fehlt.
Ein weiterer Entwurf sah für die Wohnräume große, in den Hang geschnittene Stufungen vor, durch die sich eine Terrassenfolge ergab. Die gesamte Landschaft wurde nun durch kleine Mauern, die den vertikalen Baukörper der Schlafzimmer flankierten, rhythmisch gegliedert.

Der Auftraggeber – einer der bekannten Förderer des italienischen Möbeldesigns – setzte Scarpa, nachdem er festgestellt hatte, daß er einige Termine nicht eingehalten hatte, ein Ultimatum. Als Scarpa nicht darauf einging, kündigte er den Auftrag und gab ihn an den Architekten Vico Magistretti weiter, der dann nach einem neuen Entwurf das Haus baute.

La villa Cassina est un projet tout à fait inhabituel dans l'œuvre de Scarpa. Le bâtiment devait être construit sur un terrain en pente raide et occuper aussi peu de place que possible. Scarpa dessina plusieurs solutions, utilisa des terrassements comme point de départ du travail de projection ultérieur et intégra comme il le put les pièces dans la pente. Les pièces étaient agencées sur différents niveaux le long d'un mur galbé dont la ligne domine le long corps de construction. La composition est riche en suggestions que l'on retrouve dans la villa Ottolenghi.
Des lignes polygonales qui délimitent un bassin, anticipent déjà quelques expériences constructivistes récentes, même si toute intention polémique est absente chez Scarpa.
Un autre projet prévoyait pour les pièces d'habitation de grands degrés coupés dans la pente et formant une suite de terrasses. Tout le paysage était alors rythmiquement divisé par de petits murs qui flanquaient le corps vertical de la chambre à coucher.
Le client – l'un des célèbres protecteurs du design du meuble italien – posa un ultimatum à Scarpa après avoir constaté que ce dernier n'avait pas respecté quelques dates. Comme Scarpa ne répondait pas, il résilia le contrat et passa la commande à l'architecte Vico Magistretti qui construisit alors la villa d'après un nouveau projet.

CASA BALBONI

Venice, 1964
In collaboration with: S. Los, G. Soccol

Scarpa did not complete the reconstruction and refurbishing of this Venetian house. It is a long two-storey building, with one short side facing the Grand Canal, the other looking on-to a garden. Scarpa wanted the light from the water and the garden to be exploited to the utmost as a light continuum. He therefore made use of a spiral staircase, built two open-ings to link the storeys visually, and chose clear light colours. On the canal side, the stairs, built of Lasa marble, lead from the liv-ing room to a guest suite and another living room. To the garden side, two rooms were added, roofed by a terrace to increase the space available.

Umbau und Renovierung der Casa Balboni wurden von Scarpa nicht zu Ende geführt. Es handelt sich bei diesem venezianischen Wohnhaus um ein längliches Gebäude mit zwei Stockwerken, dessen Schmalseiten ei-nerseits auf den Canal Grande, andererseits auf einen Garten blickten. Scarpa war be-müht, das Licht, das von der Wasser- bezie-hungsweise Gartenseite her einfällt, optimal auszunutzen und in einem Lichtkontinuum entsprechend zu regulieren. Zu diesem Zweck verwendete er die offene Wendeltrep-pe, fügte zwei Durchblicke ein, um so die Stockwerke optisch miteinander zu verbin-den, und wählte klare, helle Farben. Die Treppe aus Lasa-Marmor führt vom Wohn-zimmer auf der Kanalseite zu einer Gästesuite und einem weiteren Wohnraum. An der Gar-tenseite wurden zwei Räume angebaut, über-dacht von einer Terrasse, um die Grundfläche zu erweitern.

La transformation et la rénovation de la Casa Balboni ne furent pas achevées par Scarpa. Cette maison d'habitation vénitienne est un bâtiment allongé de deux étages dont les pe-tits côtés donnent d'une part sur le Canal Grande, d'autre part sur un jardin. Scarpa s'est efforcé d'utiliser au maximum la lumière qui vient de l'eau et du jardin et de la corriger en conséquence dans un continuum de lu-mière. Il a employé à cet effet l'escalier en colimaçon ouvert, réalisé deux ouvertures pour relier optiquement les étages entre eux, et choisi des couleurs claires et lumineuses. L'escalier en marbre de Lasa mène de la salle de séjour, du côté du canal, à une suite réser-vée aux visiteurs et à une autre salle de séjour. Côté jardin, on a construit deux pièces cou-vertes d'une terrasse pour agrandir la surface habitable.

CASA DE BENEDETTI-BONAIUTO

Rome, 1965–1972
In collaboration with: F. Motterle, C. Maschietto,
S. Los, E. Vittoria

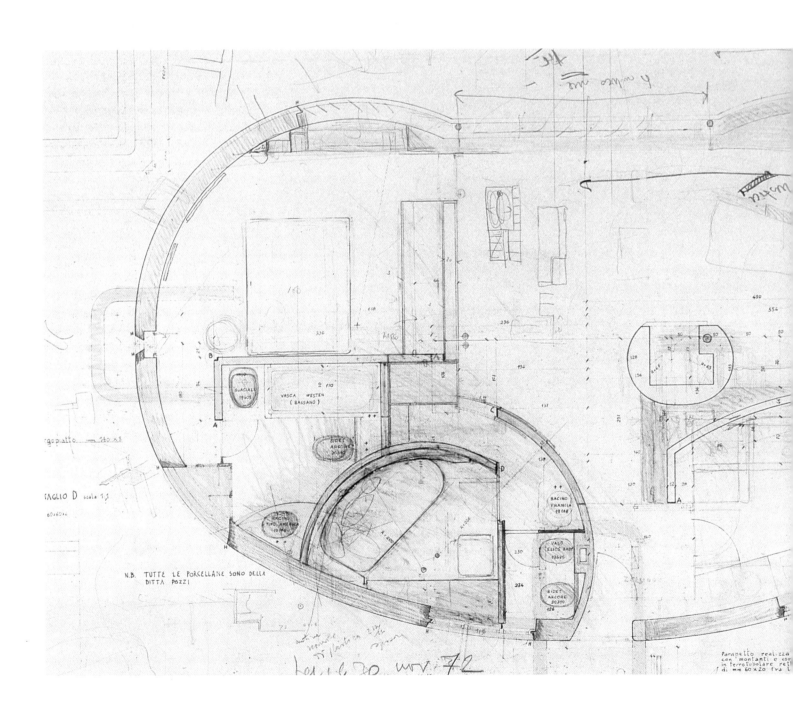

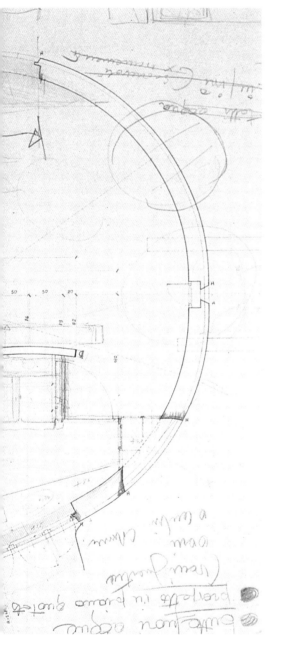

This project was intended to include the restoration of a seventeenth-century Roman villa on the Via Salaria as well as the building of a small new house in the adjacent park. Scarpa concentrated first on the new house, which he visualized as a costly étui, like a Venetian snuff box, for example.

Scarpa drew a house set on a plinth, with one large space and identifiable but continuous areas, as in Ludwig Mies van der Rohe's houses. He steadily worked away at a basic design consisting of different circles, and finally arrived at a project which reminded him of the architecture of Borromini. The support for the roof, itself a kind of shield pointing at the sky, was to have the minimum possible effect on the ground-plan. Scarpa wanted to solve this problem with slim cylindrical double columns to be made out of steel.

Intended for an elderly lady, the mother of a lawyer named De Benedetti, this simple house was designed with only one storey. The entrance was intended to be a sort of bridge, a sloping platform between the trees.

The whole composition depended on the contrast between a pavilion on the first floor, with rounded lines borrowed from Roman baroque, and the ground floor informed by Neo-Plasticism.

Dieses Projekt sollte sowohl die Restaurierung einer römischen Villa aus dem 17. Jahrhundert an der Via Salaria als auch den Neubau eines kleinen Wohnhauses im angrenzenden Park umfassen. Scarpas Entwurf konzentrierte sich zunächst auf den Neubau des Hauses, das er sich wie ein wertvolles Kästchen, eine venezianische Tabaksdose etwa, vorstellte.

Scarpa zeichnete einen Pavillon, auf einen Sockel gesetzt, mit einem einzigen großen Raum – wie in den Häusern Ludwig Mies van der Rohes: zwar mit identifizierbaren Raumeinheiten, aber doch zusammenhängend. Ständig feilte er an der Grundform, die sich aus unterschiedlichen Kreisen zusammensetzte, um schließlich einen Entwurf zu erhalten, der ihn an die Architektur von Borromini aus dem 17. Jahrhundert erinnerte. Die tragende Struktur für das Dach, eine Art zum Himmel gerichteter Schild, sollte die Organisation des Grundrisses so wenig wie möglich stören. Scarpa wollte dieses Problem mit schlanken zylindrischen Doppelstahlsäulen lösen.

Da dieses Haus für eine ältere Dame, die Mutter des Rechtsanwalts De Benedetti, gedacht war, wurde lediglich ein Stockwerk geplant. Als Zugang sollte eine Art Brücke, eine schräge Rampe zwischen den Bäumen, dienen.

Die gesamte Komposition stützte sich auf den Kontrast zwischen Pavillon einerseits, der, in Anlehnung an das römische Barock, gerundeten Linien folgte, und der Innenraumgestaltung andererseits, die dem Neoplastizismus verpflichtet war.

Ce projet comprenait la restauration d'une villa romaine du XVIIe siécle dans la Via Salaria et la nouvelle construction d'une petite maison d'habitation dans le parc avoisinant. Le plan de Scarpa se concentra avant toute chose sur le nouveau bâtiment qu'il se représentait comme une petite boîte précieuse, peut-être une tabatière vénitienne.

Scarpa dessina un pavillon posé sur un socle, avec une salle unique de vastes dimensions – comme dans les maisons de Ludwig Mies van der Rohe, avec des espaces diversifiés, mais continue. Il fignolait constamment la forme primitive qui était composée de différents cercles et finit par obtenir un projet qui lui rappelait l'architecture de Borromini, au XVIIe siècle. La structure portante pour le toit, sorte de bouclier tourné vers le ciel, devait entraver aussi peu que possible l'aménagement du plan d'ensemble. Scarpa voulait résoudre ce problème à l'aide de minces colonnes géminées métalliques en forme de cylindre.

Prévue pour une femme âgée, la mère de l'avocat De Benedetti, cette simple maison fut conçue avec un seul étage. Une sorte de pont, un plan incliné entre les arbres, devait y accéder. Toute la composition s'appuyait sur le contraste existant entre le pavillon, d'une part, qui suit des lignes arrondies sur le modèle du baroque romain, et de l'aménagement intérieur d'autre part, qui doit beaucoup au Néo-plasticisme.

FONDAZIONE MASIERI

Venice (1970), 1983
In collaboration with: C. Maschietto, F. Semi

The chequered history of the Masieri Foundation building, now a Galleria di Architettura, dates from Scarpa's cooperation with the young Friulian architect Angelo Masieri, who, like Scarpa, believed that architecture should follow Frank Lloyd Wright. Some projects from these years, for example the bank at Tarvisio and a villa at Cervignano, illustrate their joint search for the new concept of space which characterized organic architecture at the time.

Angelo Masieri died after a car accident in the USA in 1952. In his memory, his parents commissioned Frank Lloyd Wright, whom he had never met, to design a building on the Grand Canal in Venice, where they owned a small plot of land. This was to house a foundation under the aegis of the Istituto Universitario di Architettura di Venezia.

Wright's project aroused furious controversy and none dared to take it up. Scarpa's hopes that planning consent might after all be granted a few years later were not realized. In 1962 the Foundation commissioned Valeriano Pastor to draw up a new plan with precise instructions on the conservation of the existing structure, but without success. So it was left to Scarpa to investigate the possibilities of converting the building into a students' hostel. Between 1968 and 1970 he put forward various draft proposals, but these found little favour, especially in the matter of the façade overlooking the Grand Canal. However, a revised project was accepted in 1973 after some delay.

After Scarpa's death the building remained a half-finished skeleton until his former collaborator, Maschietto, and the architect Semi completed it in 1983.

Das Gebäude der Masieri-Stiftung, das zur Zeit als Galleria di Architettura dient, hat eine wechselvolle Entstehungsgeschichte, deren Beginn in eine Zeit fällt, als Scarpa mit dem jungen friaulischen Architekten Angelo Masieri zusammenarbeitete. Beide vertraten die Auffassung, daß die neue Architektur dem Vorbild Frank Lloyd Wrights folgen sollte. Einige Projekte aus diesen Jahren, die Bank von Tarvisio und eine Villa in Cervignano beispielsweise, sind Ausdruck ihrer gemeinsamen Suche nach jener neuen Raumkonzeption, die die organische Architektur damals kennzeichnete.

Auf einer Reise durch die USA starb Angelo Masieri 1952 an den Folgen eines Autounfalls. Zum Gedenken an ihren Sohn beauftragten seine Eltern Frank Lloyd Wright, mit dem er nicht mehr hatte zusammentreffen können, mit dem Entwurf eines Gebäudes, das am Canal Grande in Venedig stehen sollte, wo sie ein kleines Grundstück besaßen. Es sollte eine Stiftung unter der Leitung der Architekturfakultät von Venedig beherbergen.

Wrights Entwurf löste heftige Diskussionen aus, und keiner hatte den Mut, die Verantwortung für die Realisierung des Projekts zu übernehmen. Auch Scarpas Hoffnung, vielleicht in einigen Jahren doch noch eine Baugenehmigung zu erreichen, zerschlug sich.

1962 beauftragte die Stiftung Valeriano Pastor mit einem neuen Entwurf, mit genauen Vorgaben, was die Erhaltung der vorhandenen Bausubstanz anging. Die Planung wurde jedoch nicht abgeschlossen. So blieb es Scarpa vorbehalten, nach Möglichkeiten einer Umgestaltung des Gebäudes in ein Studentenheim zu suchen. Zwischen 1968 und 1970 entwickelte er verschiedene Projektentwürfe, die jedoch auf wenig Akzeptanz stießen, vor allem was die Fassade zum Canal Grande hin anbetraf. Nach einer nochmaligen Überarbeitung und etlichem Hin und Her wurde der Umbau 1973 schließlich genehmigt.

Nach dem Tod Scarpas blieb das Haus zunächst halbfertig im Rohbau stehen und wurde erst 1983 von seinem ehemaligen Mitarbeiter Maschietto fertiggestellt.

L'édifice de la fondation Masieri, qui sert actuellement de Galleria di Architectura, a une histoire mouvementée; celle-ci remonte à l'époque où Scarpa collaborait avec le jeune architecte frioulien Angelo Masieri. Tous deux pensaient que la nouvelle architecture devait suivre l'exemple de Frank Lloyd Wright. Quelques projets conçus à cette époque, par exemple la banque de Tarvisio et une villa à Cervignano, expriment leur commune recherche de la conception spatiale qui caractérisait alors l'architecture organique.

Angelo Masieri mourut des suites d'un accident de voiture, alors qu'il effectuait un voyage aux USA. En mémoire de leur fils, ses parents chargèrent Frank Lloyd Wright, qu'il n'avait pas pu rencontrer, d'ébaucher un bâtiment qui devait être construit au bord du Canal Grande à Venise où ils possédaient un petit terrain. Ce bâtiment devait abriter une fondation placée sous la direction de la faculté d'architecture de Venise.

Le projet de Wright déclencha de violentes discussions et personne n'eut le courage d'assumer la responsabilité de la réalisation du projet. Scarpa, qui pensait pourtant obtenir un permis de construire quelques années plus tard, vit également ses espoirs réduits à néant. En 1962, la fondation Masieri chargea Valeriano Pastor d'exécuter une nouvelle ébauche, avec des directives précises en ce qui concerne le maintien de la substance architectonique. La planification ne fut toutefois pas terminée. Scarpa dut donc chercher des possibilités pour transformer le bâtiment en foyer d'étudiants. Entre 1968 et 1970, il élabora plusieurs projets qui furent toutefois difficilement acceptés, surtout en ce qui concerne la façade donnant sur le Canal Grande. Après de nouvelles retouches et bien des discussions, la transformation fut finalement autorisée en 1973.

Après la mort de Scarpa, le bâtiment resta d'abord à moitié fini, à l'état de gros œuvre, et fut seulement achevé par son ancien collaborateur Maschietto en 1983.

128

BRION FAMILY CEMETERY

San Vito d'Altivole, Treviso, 1969–1978
In collaboration with: G. Pietropoli, C. Maschietto

»Someone died, here in Italy, and the family wanted to commemorate the achievements of this person, who came from a humble background – ›dalla gavetta‹ as we say – and who, through his work, attained a certain importance... In fact a mere 100 square metres would have sufficed but I was given 2200 square metres... Well, I did what you have seen.

The monument or the sarcophagi were to stand here on an exposed site, with a panorama. The deceased wanted to be close to the earth of the village where he was born. So I had the idea of building a small arch which I call the ›arcosolium‹, a Latin term used by the early Christians. In the catacombs, important people or martyrs were given a more lavish tomb, called an ›arcosolium‹, but it amounted to no more than a simple arch, like this.

It is beautiful when two people who have loved each other in life continue to bow in mutual greeting in death. They should not be erect: that would be for soldiers. So an arch was built, a bridge made of reinforced concrete. But, to take away the impression of a bridge, the arch had to be decorated, the vault painted. My arch I covered in mosaic, a Venetian tradition which I interpreted in my own way.

The great cypress avenue leading to the graveyard is an Italian tradition, it is a sort of race track, a wide, long road. Architects have had enough of these race tracks. This road is called the ›propylaeum‹ after the Greek word for entrance, and that is the ›portico‹, a colonnade. This is the starting point. These two eyes determine the view. The site was just too large; it gave the feeling of a meadow. To justify the large area it seemed sensible to me to build a little temple for funeral services – ›burial‹ is such a terrible word.

But the area was still too large, so we raised the ground level to be able to see outside. So one can look out but nothing can be seen from outside. Here are the tombstone, the graves of the family, the little temple, the altar.

»Ein Mensch starb, hier in Italien; die Familie wollte das Verdienst dieses Menschen ehren, der aus einfachen Verhältnissen – ›dalla gavetta‹, wie wir hier sagen – kam und durch seine Arbeit einige Bedeutung erlangt hatte... Eigentlich hätten mir 100 Quadratmeter gereicht, statt dessen waren es 2200... Nun, ich habe es dann so gemacht, wie ihr es gesehen habt.

Das Grabmal oder die Sarkophage, wie man sagen könnte, sollten hier stehen, an einer exponierten Stelle: Von hier aus also ein Panoramablick. Der Verstorbene wollte der Erde dieses Dorfes, in dem er geboren wurde, nahe sein. So kam mir die Idee, einen kleinen Bogen zu bauen, den ich ›arcosolium‹ nenne, ein lateinischer Begriff aus frühchristlicher Zeit. In den Katakomben wurden wichtige Personen oder Märtyrer aufwendiger begraben; man nannte das dann ›arcosolium‹ – das hier ist nur so ein einfacher Bogen.

Es ist etwas Schönes, wenn sich zwei Menschen, die sich im Leben geliebt haben, nach dem Tode zum Gruß einander zuneigen. Sie sollten nicht aufrecht stehen; das ist die Haltung der Soldaten. So entstand ein Bogen, eine Brücke – eine Brücke aus Eisenbeton; ein Bogen aus Eisenbeton wäre jedoch nur Brücke geblieben: Um den Eindruck der Brücke aufzuheben, mußte man den Bogen schmücken, seine Wölbung bemalen. Ich habe dafür Mosaik gewählt, das zur venezianischen Tradition gehört, allerdings auf meine Weise interpretiert.

Die große Zypressenallee, die zum Friedhof führt, entspricht italienischer Tradition; sie ist eine Art Rennstrecke, ein breit angelegter und langer Weg. Die Architekten haben genug von diesen Rennstrecken. Dieser Weg hier nennt sich ›Propyläen‹, das heißt auf griechisch: Tür, Eingang – und das da ist der ›Portikus‹, der Säulengang. Das ist der Ausgangspunkt: Diese beiden Augen bestimmen den Blick. Von daher war das Gelände einfach zu groß – es wurde zur Wiese. Um die große Fläche zu rechtfertigen, erschien es mir sinnvoll, einen kleinen Tempel für Trauerfeiern – ›Begräbnis‹ ist so ein schreckliches Wort – dorthin zu bauen.

Das Ganze war aber immer noch zu groß; da haben wir den Boden etwas angehoben, damit man nach draußen sehen kann. Ich kann also nach draußen blicken, von draußen aber nicht hineinsehen. Hier sind das Grabmal, die Gräber der Familie und der Angehörigen, der kleine Tempel, der Altar.

«Une personne est morte, ici en Italie; la famille voulait honorer les services rendus par ladite personne qui était d'humble origine – ‹dalla gavetta›, comme on dit ici – et était parvenue à une certaine importance par son travail... Cent mètres carrés m'auraient suffi, au lieu de cela, il y en avait deux mille deux cents. Alors j'ai fait ce que vous avez vu.

Le tombeau ou le sarcophage, comme on pourrait dire, devait se trouver à cet endroit, à un emplacement exposé: la vue devait donc être panoramique à partir de là. Le défunt voulait être proche de la terre du village où il était né. J'ai donc eu l'idée de construire un petit arc que j'appelle ‹arcosolium›, notion latine des débuts du christianisme. Dans les catacombes, les importants personnages ou les martyrs étaient enterrés à grands frais, on appelait cela ‹arcosolium› – ceci n'est qu'un simple arc.

Quand deux êtres qui se sont aimés de leur vivant se penchent l'un vers l'autre pour se donner le bonjour après leur mort, c'est très beau. Ils ne devaient pas être debout, car c'est la position des soldats. C'est ainsi qu'est né un arc, un pont, un pont en béton armé; un arc en béton armé serait seulement resté un pont: pour conserver l'impression de pont, il a fallu orner l'arc, peindre sa voûte. J'ai choisi à cet effet la mosaïque, qui fait partie de la tradition vénitienne, et l'ai, à vrai dire, interprétée à ma manière.

La grande allée de cyprès qui mène au cimetière correspond à la tradition italienne, c'est une sorte de parcours, un chemin à la fois long et large. Les architectes ne veulent plus de ces parcours. Ce chemin s'appelle ‹propylée›, c'est-à-dire porte, entrée, en grec, et voilà le ‹portique›, le péristyle. C'est le point de départ: ces deux yeux déterminent la vue. Pour cette raison, le terrain était bien trop vaste – il est devenu prairie. Pour justifier la grande surface, il m'a semblé judicieux d'y construire un petit temple pour les funérailles – ‹enterrement› est un mot tellement affreux. Cependant, le tout était encore trop grand; nous avons donc légèrement rehaussé le sol, afin que l'on puisse voir à l'extérieur. Je peux donc voir à l'extérieur toutefois, je ne peux pas voir à l'intérieur. Le tombeau, les tombes de la famille et des proches, le petit temple et l'autel sont là.

Corner of the boundary wall from inside (below);
view from the drive to the municipal cemetery
(right page)

From the village the site is approached
through a private entrance; here is the church,
where funeral services are held, the village
cemetery, and here is the chapel – this is accessible to the public because the ground belongs to the estate. The family has the right
only to be buried there. A private path leads to
the little pavilion on the water – the only really private area on the site. That is basically all
there is. This place of the dead is a little like a
garden. Incidentally, the great American
cemeteries of the nineteenth century, in
Chicago, for example, are extensive parks. No
Napoleonic tomb, no! You can drive in with
your car. There are beautiful monuments, for
example those by Louis Henry Sullivan.
Cemeteries now have become mere piled-up
shoe boxes, one on top of the other. I wanted
to express the naturalness of water and
meadow, of water and earth. Water is the
source of life.«

Apart from the fact that the description by
Scarpa quoted at length here explains his
motives and preferences as an architect, it re-
minds those who knew him of his ironical way
of speaking about architecture. His lectures
were charming conversations quite devoid of
any academic tone.

Scarpa designed the Brion tomb during the
student revolt in Italian universities. Architecture was forgotten, politically irrelevant. Scarpa was director of the Venice faculty, an insti-
tute which no one at the time wanted to run.
But his friendly manner disarmed the ubiquit-
ous aggressiveness of the demogogues.

The site is an L-shape situated along two sides
of the cemetery of San Vito. A boundary wall
leaning inwards encloses the site with its three
centres: the pool around the pavilion, the »arcosolium« at the corner of the »L«, and the
chapel. There are two entrances, one directly
from outside to the chapel, the other from the
cemetery at the end of the main avenue. This
second entrance gives access to the site; Scarpa borrowed the name »propylaeum« from
the Acropolis. It leads to a portico, from
which one sees the garden through two in-
tersecting mosaic-framed rings.

Vom Dorf her betritt man das Areal durch einen eigenen Eingang, hier die Kirche, der Ort
der Trauerfeier, der Friedhof des Dorfes und
hier die Kapelle – diese steht der Öffentlich-
keit zur Verfügung, da der Grund staatlich ist.
Die Familie hat nur das Recht, dort begraben
zu werden. Hier befindet sich ein privater
Weg, der bis zu dem kleinen Pavillon auf dem
Wasser führt – das einzig wirklich Private auf
dem Gelände. Das ist im großen und ganzen
alles. Der Ort der Toten hat etwas von einem
Garten; übrigens sind die großen amerikani-
schen Friedhöfe des 19. Jahrhunderts, in Chicago etwa, weitläufige Parkanlagen. Kein napoleonischer Friedhof, nein! Man kann dort
mit dem Auto hineinfahren. Es gibt schöne
Grabmäler, zum Beispiel von Louis Henry
Sullivan. Jetzt sind die Friedhöfe nur noch
Schuhschachtelhaufen, Stück für Stück auf-
einandergestapelt . . . Ich wollte vielmehr das
Natürliche von Wasser und Wiese, von Wasser und Erde zum Ausdruck bringen: Wasser
ist die Quelle des Lebens.«

Abgesehen davon, daß diese ausführlich zitierte Beschreibung Scarpas seine Motive und
Präferenzen deutlich macht, erinnert sie zugleich diejenigen, die ihn kannten, an seine
ironische Art, über Architektur zu sprechen.
Seine Vorlesungen waren liebenswürdige Un-
terhaltungen, die frei waren von jeglichem
akademischen Ton.

Scarpa plante das Grabmal Brion, als an den
italienischen Universitäten die Studentenre-
volte ausgebrochen war. Die Architektur blieb
dabei als nicht politisch relevant im Abseits.
Scarpa war damals Direktor einer Fakultät,
deren Leitung zu jener Zeit keiner übernehmen wollte. Ihm jedoch gelang es, in aller
Freundlichkeit der allgegenwärtigen Demago-
gie und Aggressivität zu widerstehen.

Das Areal, auf dem das Monument steht, be-
schreibt die Form eines L um zwei Seiten des
Friedhofs von San Vito. Eine nach innen ge-
neigte Einfriedungsmauer begrenzt das Gelände und markiert drei zentrale Orte: das Wasserbecken mit dem Pavillon, das »arcosolium« im Winkel des L und die Kapelle. Es gibt
zwei Eingänge: einen direkt von außen, zur
Kapelle hin; den anderen vom Friedhof her,
am Ende der Hauptallee. Durch diesen zweiten Eingang, durch den wir das Areal betreten
und den Scarpa in Anlehnung an die Akropo-
lis »Propyläen« nannte, gelangt man zu einem
Portikus, von dem aus man durch die beiden
sich überschneidenden Kreise mit Mosaikrah-
men den Garten sieht.

Approach to the Brion family tomb from the
municipal cemetery (below); detail of the inter-
secting circles in the portico (left page)

View of the pool with the pavilion (below);
corner of the portico, with mosaic decoration
(right page)

A partir du village, on pénètre dans le site par une petite entrée; ici l'église, le lieu des obsèques, le cimetière du village et là la chapelle – qui est à la disposition du public, puisque le terrain appartient à l'Etat. La famille a seulement l'autorisation d'être enterrée à cet endroit. Ici se trouve un chemin privé qui mène à un petit pavillon sur l'eau – la seule chose vraiment privée sur ce terrain. En gros, c'est tout. Le lieu où reposent les morts a un air de jardin; d'ailleurs, les grands cimetières américains du XIXe siècle, par exemple celui de Chicago, sont de vastes parcs. Pas un cimetière napoléonien, non! On peut y entrer en voiture. Il y a de beaux tombeaux, par exemple celui de Louis Henry Sullivan. Maintenant, les cimetières ne sont plus que des tas de boîtes à chaussures entassées les unes sur les autres . . . Je voulais au contraire exprimer le naturel de l'eau et de la prairie: l'eau est la source de la vie.»

Mis à part le fait que cette description détaillée de Scarpa montre nettement les motifs et les préférences de l'architecte, elle rappelle en même temps à ceux qui le connaissaient la façon ironique dont il parlait de l'architecture. Ses cours étaient en effet d'aimables conversations dépourvues de tout académisme. Scarpa réalisa le plan du tombeau de la famille Brion au moment où la révolte des étudiants éclatait dans les universités italiennes. L'architecture resta à l'écart, n'ayant pas une importance politique. Scarpa était alors recteur d'une faculté dont personne à l'époque ne voulait assumer la direction. Il parvint toutefois à résister à la démagogie et à l'agressivité omniprésentes.

Le site sur lequel se trouve le monument est en forme de L et longe deux côtés du cimetière de San Vito. Un mur d'enceinte incliné vers l'intérieur limite le terrain et accentue trois lieux essentiels: le bassin avec le pavillon, l'«arcosolium» dans l'angle du L et la chapelle. Il y a deux entrées, la première vient directement de l'extérieur, vers la chapelle, l'autre du cimetière, au bout de l'allée principale. Par cette deuxième entrée, à travers laquelle nous pénétrons dans le site et que Scarpa a appelée «propylée» sur le modèle de l'Acropole, on parvient à un portique, à partir duquel on voit le jardin à travers deux cercles encadrés de mosaïque.

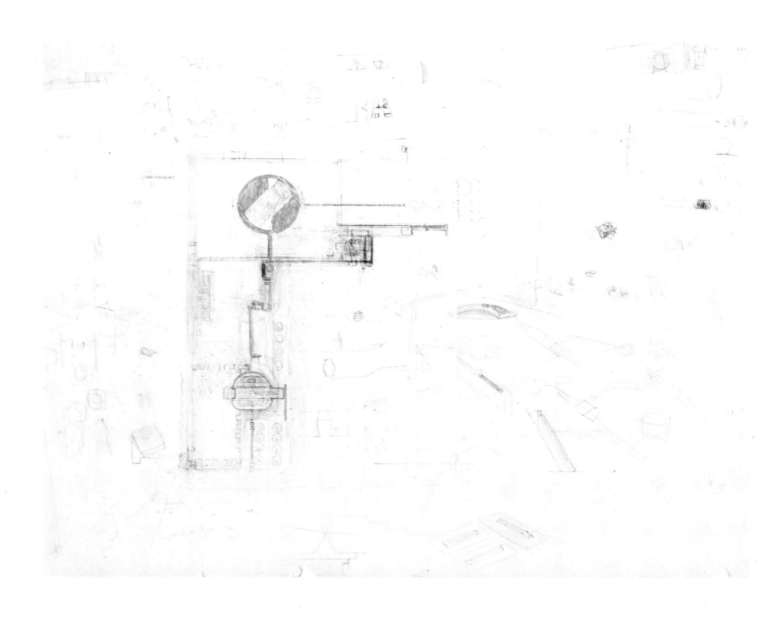

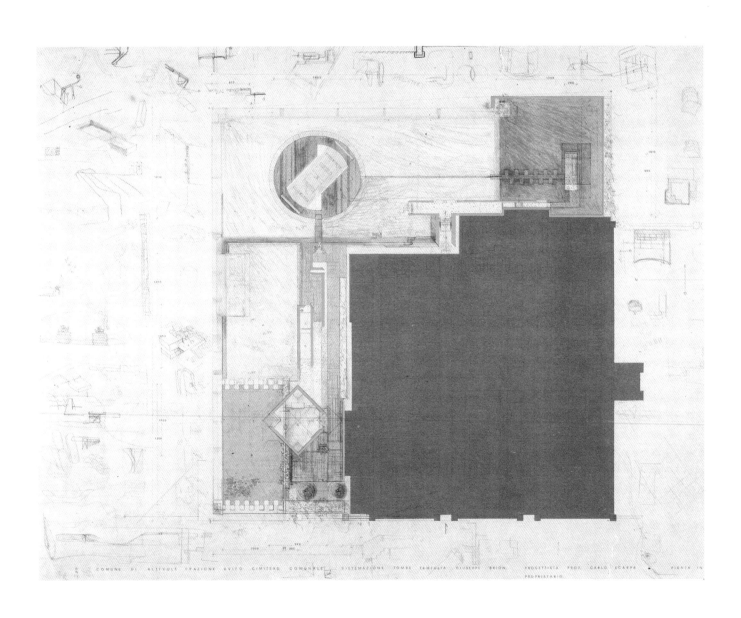

Preliminary sketch and final drawing for the
Brion Family Cemetery

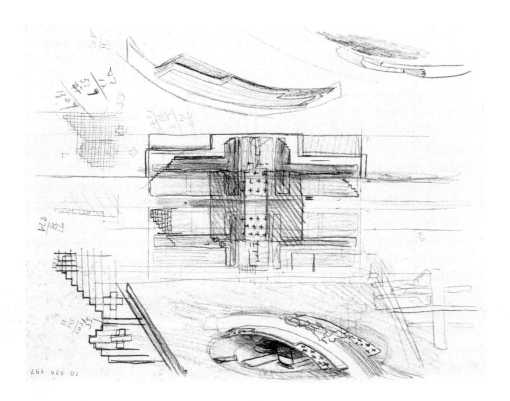

To the right the visitor sees the only area closed to the public – the pavilion of meditation surrounded by a pool. Its glass access door is operated by counterweights and rollers visible from outside. Between the water lilies in the pool an emblem can be seen, a cruciform maze. The water is led off into a little brook that ends near the tombs. At a lower level, overhung by the »arcosolium«, are the two tombs of light and dark stone. They support a shrine of jacaranda wood in which the names are inscribed in ebony and ivory. To the side in the meadow are the graves of the family under a roof, which, while heavy, seems almost to float.

Rechts vom Eingang befindet sich der einzige private Ort, zu dem Besucher keinen Zugang haben: der Pavillon der Meditation, in der Mitte eines Wasserbeckens gelegen. Die Bedienung der Glastür, die den Durchgang versperrt, geschieht durch Gegengewichte und Rollen, die von außen sichtbar sind. Zwischen den Seerosen im Becken ist ein Emblem zu sehen: ein Kreuzlabyrinth. Das Wasser geht dann in ein Bächlein über, das dort endet, wo die Sarkophage stehen. An einer tiefergelegenen Stelle und geschützt durch das »arcosolium«, befinden sich die beiden Grabmäler aus hellem und dunklem Stein. Sie tragen einen Schrein aus Palisander, in den die Namen mit Ebenholz und Elfenbein eingeschrieben sind. Etwas abseits, auf der Wiese, liegen die Gräber der Angehörigen unter einem schweren, doch fast schwebenden Dach.

A droite, en entrant, se trouve le seul endroit privé où le visiteur ne peut entrer, à savoir le pavillon de méditation situé au milieu d'un bassin. L'ouverture de la porte vitrée, qui barre le passage, se fait au moyen de contrepoids et de poulies visibles de l'extérieur. Entre les nénuphars du bassin, on voit un emblème: un labyrinthe en croix. L'eau passe ensuite dans un petit ruisseau qui se termine là où sont les sarcophages. Les deux tombeaux en pierre claire et sombre se trouvent à un endroit moins élevé et protégé par l'«arcosolium»; ils supportent un coffre en palissandre sur lequel les noms sont inscrits en bois d'ébène et en ivoire. Les tombes des proches sont placées un peu en dehors, dans la prairie, sous un toit lourd et néanmoins presque flottant.

At the end of the garden we come to the chapel, which is directly connected to the cemetery drive via an iron-framed concrete gate. The chapel is rectangular, set in plan at 45 degrees to the enclosing wall, and dominated by an indentation motif. Surrounded by water and cypress trees, this is the last episode of a place with an oriental yet deeply Venetian atmosphere, where one would gladly see children playing on the grass. Nothing disturbs the evocative intensity of the pure architecture. In a corner of the garden, a tomb designed by Scarpa's son, Tobia, is a reminder that the architect is buried here.

Am Ende der Anlage gelangt man zur Kapelle, die über ein eisengefaßtes Betontor auch direkt mit der Zufahrt zum Friedhof verbunden ist. Die Kapelle ist rechteckig und, bezogen auf die Umfassungsmauer des Geländes, um 45 Grad gedreht, aus Beton und vom Thema der Zackenprofile beherrscht. Von Wasser und Zypressen umgeben, ist es die letzte Episode eines Ortes von orientalischer und doch zutiefst venezianischer Atmosphäre. Man würde dort gerne Kinder auf der Wiese spielen sehen. Nichts stört die evokative Intensität der reinen Architektur. In einer Ecke der Anlage erinnert das von Scarpas Sohn Tobia entworfene Grab daran, daß hier der Architekt begraben wurde.

Au bout du parc, on parvient à une chapelle directement reliée à l'accès du cimetière par un porche en béton armé. La chapelle rectangulaire est tournée de 45 degrés par rapport au mur d'enceinte du terrain. Elle est en béton et dominée par le thème des dentelures. Entourée d'eau et de cyprès, c'est la dernière réalisation d'un lieu où règne une atmosphère orientale et pourtant profondément vénitienne. On aimerait voir des enfants en train de jouer dans la prairie. Rien ne dérange l'intensité évocatrice de l'architecture pure. Dans un coin du site, la tombe réalisée par Tobia, le fils de Scarpa, rappelle que l'architecte est enterré en cet endroit.

During funeral services, a double door behind the
altar can be opened; the pool behind reflects additional
light into the interior; design and execution

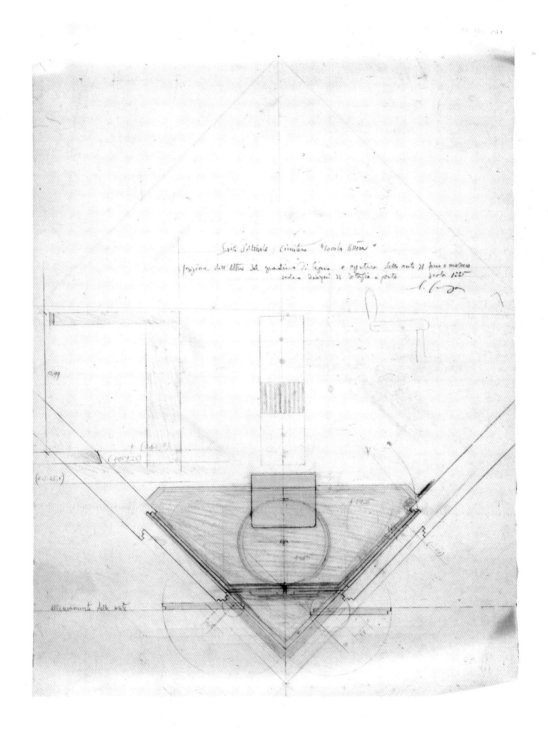

BANCA POPOLARE DI VERONA

Verona, 1973–1981
In collaboration with: A. Rudi

Carlo Scarpa's extension of the Banca Popolare di Verona is on the site of two demolished buildings next to the existing bank, which is still in use. The project underwent many changes over the years both as a result of the client's new specifications and of the architect's fresh thoughts. Continual revision and critical examination, which often led to unexpected results, were important to his method of working. This »filing down« was a process of small corrections leading to the final shape of the whole project; according to Scarpa, just like a woman's face, which would lose its charisma and harmony were but a slight change made to its proportions or to a single detail.

The main themes of the project did not change: a forward-thrusting front elevation, constructed on the classical three principles of plinth, middle part and cornice. Originally the rear elevation was provided with continuous horizontal bands, unlike the front, but the two are now basically similar.

When Scarpa suddenly died in November 1978, the building was broadly complete. The front and rear elevations facing the Piazza and the courtyard were built, and much of the material for interior fittings had been ordered. Arrigo Rudi, who had worked on the project throughout, including its construction, saw it through to a successful conclusion.

The façades are among the most interesting parts of the work. The window panes stand either well behind the wall slabs, which are plastered with »cocciopesto«, a mixture of lime and brick chippings, or they project from the surface like crystal shrines. The circular windows have different diameters, a trick used by Scarpa to achieve liveliness.

Der von Carlo Scarpa gestaltete Erweiterungsbau der Banca Popolare di Verona steht an Stelle zweier abgerissener Gebäude direkt neben dem bisherigen Sitz, der immer noch genutzt wird. Das Projekt erfuhr im Laufe der Jahre zahlreiche Veränderungen, sowohl aufgrund neuer Vorgaben von seiten der Auftraggeber als auch aufgrund neuer Überlegungen des Architekten. Die kontinuierliche Überarbeitung und kritische Überprüfung des Entwurfs, die häufig zu unerwarteten Ergebnissen führten, waren ganz entscheidende Elemente seiner Arbeitsweise. Es handelte sich um jene »Arbeit mit der Feile«, die mit Hilfe kleiner Korrekturen den Gesamtentwurf in seine endgültige Form bringen sollte – gleichsam wie das Gesicht einer Frau, so sagte Scarpa, das seine Ausstrahlung, seine Harmonie verlieren würde, wenn man es nur ein wenig in seinen Proportionen oder nur in einem Detail verändern würde.

Konstant blieben die wesentlichen Themen des Entwurfs: die vorgesetzte Fassade und der Aufbau nach der klassischen Dreiteilung in Sockel, Mittelteil und Bekrönung. Die rückseitige Fassade unterschied sich ursprünglich von der Hauptfassade: Sie war mit durchgehend horizontalen Bändern versehen, während sie jetzt die gleichen Merkmale aufweist wie die Vorderfront.

Beim plötzlichen Tode Scarpas im November 1978 war der Bau in allen Teilen schon in groben Zügen ausgeführt; vollständig fertiggestellt waren die beiden Fassaden, zur Piazza und zum Hof hin. Arrigo Rudi, der das Projekt in allen seinen Phasen und die Bauarbeiten bis zu diesem Zeitpunkt begleitet hatte, setzte die angefangene Arbeit fort und führte sie zu einem gelungenen Abschluß.

Die Fassaden gehören zu den interessantesten Elementen dieses Bauwerks. Die Fensterebenen liegen entweder deutlich hinter den mit »cocciopesto«, einer Mischung aus Kalk und Ziegelsplitt, verputzten Wandscheiben oder treten deutlich hervor und sitzen wie Kristallschreine auf der Fläche. Die ausgeschnittenen Kreise haben unterschiedliche Radien, ein Kunstgriff, den Scarpa anwendete, um das Motiv dynamischer zu gestalten.

L'annexe de la Banca Popolare di Verona conçue par Scarpa est située à la place de deux bâtiments rasés, juste à côté de l'ancien siège social qui est toujours utilisé. Au cours des ans, le projet a subi de nombreuses modifications, aussi bien à cause des nouvelles exigences des clients qu'à cause des nouvelles réflexions de l'architecte. Les retouches continuelles et l'examen critique du projet, qui aboutissaient souvent à des résultats inattendus, ont été les éléments décisifs de sa méthode de travail. Il s'agissait là du «fignolage» qui devait donner au projet d'ensemble sa forme définitive au moyen de petites corrections – en quelque sorte comme le visage d'une femme qui, comme disait Scarpa, perdrait son rayonnement et son harmonie, si l'on changeait quoi que ce soit à ses proportions ou même à un seul détail.

Les thèmes essentiels du projet sont restés constants: façade avancée et construction conforme à la division classique en trois parties, à savoir socle, partie médiane et couronnement. La façade arrière était à l'origine différente de la façade principale: elle était en effet pourvue de bandes horizontales continues, alors qu'elle présente désormais dans l'ensemble les mêmes caractéristiques que la façade principale.

Quand Scarpa mourut subitement en novembre 1978, la construction était déjà réalisée en gros dans toutes les parties; les deux façades, donnant sur la Piazza et sur la cour, étaient entièrement terminées, et la plupart des matériaux prévus pour l'achèvement intérieur étaient déjà commandés. Arrigo Rudi, qui avait suivi jusque-là toutes les phases du projet et les travaux de construction, continua le travail et le mena à bonne fin.

Les façades font partie des éléments les plus intéressants de cette construction. Les fenêtres se trouvent soit nettement derrière les murs crépis avec du «cocciopesto», mélange fait de chaux et de briques concassées, soit s'avancent nettement et sont assises sur la surface comme des boîtes en cristal. Les cercles découpés ont des rayons différents, un procédé que Scarpa employait afin de rendre le motif plus dynamique.

The rear façade (right); preliminary sketch for the
twin pillars (below)

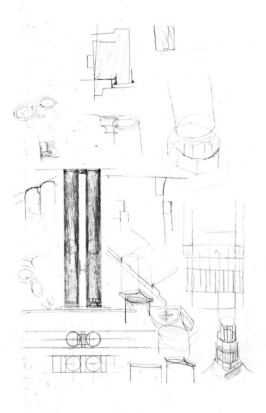

The plinth is of Botticino marble, as is the cornice. Classical motifs are quoted in its stepped cross-section. Scarpa built up this section from two courses of blocks laid one above the other. One course is set back, on the one hand to emphasize the difference between them, and on the other to keep water out. The cornice follows the Venetian tradition for the façade of a palazzo; in particular the idea of projecting surfaces on which a strong light falls was inspired mainly by elements such as those at the Fondaco dei Turchi in Venice. A red Verona marble cornice with dogtooth moulding also appears on both façades as well as over the windows and, inside, on the staircase.

The main surfaces of the façades terminate at the level of the top-floor windows, as if the bank's flat roof were floating above them. In the loggia above, the materials are different, with metal beams and columns and a frieze of coloured mosaic. The long strip of the main beam, made of two steel joists of different sizes connected by bolts and gussets, is supported at regular intervals by pairs of thin cylindrical steel columns. These double cylinders are held top and bottom by a link of Muntz metal, a brass with a high zinc content. The same hard alloy is used for other links between the small columns.

Der Sockel besteht aus Botticino-Marmor, ebenso das abschließende Kranzgesims. Es zeigt ein Stufenprofil, mit dem Scarpa Motive der klassischen Architektur zitierte. Dieses Profilmotiv wird durch zwei übereinandergeschichtete Blockreihen gebildet, die gegeneinander versetzt sind, einerseits um die beiden Reihen zu unterscheiden, andererseits um damit das Eindringen von Wasser zu verhindern. Das Gesims folgt der venezianischen Tradition der Bekrönung an den Fassaden der Palazzi: Insbesondere die Idee der vorspringenden Flächen, auf die ein intensives Licht fällt, ist angeregt durch Bekrönungen, wie die am Fondaco dei Turchi in Venedig. Ein Gesims mit Zahnschnittfries aus rotem veronesischem Marmor kehrt auch in den Bänderungen der beiden Fassaden wieder, ebenso bei den Fenstern und innen am Haupttreppenaufgang.

Die Fassadenflächen enden in Höhe der Fensterbrüstungen der letzten Etage, so, als ob das Flachdach der Bank darüberschwebte. In der abschließenden Loggia wechseln die Materialien: Träger und Stützen aus Metall, als Fries ein farbiges Mosaik. Das lange Band des Tragebalkens, der von zwei Eisenträgern un-

terschiedlicher Größe gebildet wird, die
durch Knotenbleche und Bolzen miteinander
verbunden sind, stützt sich in regelmäßigen
Abständen auf Paare von kleinen, runden Ei-
senrohrsäulen. Diese Doppelsäulchen sind
oben und unten mit einem Säulenhals aus
Muntzmetall – einer Messinglegierung mit ho-
hem Zinkanteil – versehen, der als Verbin-
dungselement fungiert. Aus der gleichen har-
ten Legierung sind auch die Verbindungsstük-
ke zwischen den kleinen Säulen.

Le socle est composé de marbre de Botticino,
de même que la corniche qui sert de finition.
Cette dernière a un profil à gradins à l'aide
duquel Scarpa a cité des motifs de l'architecture classique. Ce motif profilé est formé de
deux rangs de blocs empilés l'un sur l'autre
qui sont décalés, d'une part pour différencier
ainsi les deux rangées, d'autre part pour empêcher la pénétration de l'eau. La corniche
reprend la tradition vénitienne du couronnement sur les façades des palais: en particulier
l'idée des surfaces qui s'avancent, et sur lesquelles tombe une lumière intense, est suggé-
rée par des corniches comme celle du Fondaco dei Turchi à Venise. Une corniche avec
frise dentée en marbre rouge de Vérone revient aussi dans les bandes des deux façades
de même que dans les fenêtres et dans l'escalier principal, à l'intérieur.
Les surfaces de la façade se terminent à la
hauteur des appuis de fenêtre du dernier
étage, comme si le toit plat de la banque flot-
tait dessus. Dans la loggia au-dessus, les matériaux changent: supports et piliers métalliques, frise en mosaïque colorée. La longue
bande de la poutre maîtresse, qui est constituée par deux poutrelles en fer de différentes
dimensions reliées par des couvre-joints et des
boulons, s'appuie à intervalles réguliers sur
des paires de colonnes en tubes métalliques.
Ces doubles colonnes sont pourvues, en haut
et en bas, d'un col de colonne en métal de
Muntz – alliage de laiton contenant un haut
pourcentage de zinc –, qui sert d'élément de
liaison. Les pièces de jonction entre les petites
colonnes sont également fabriquées avec le
même alliage dur.

Staircase tower (left page); detail of the twin
pillars (right)

Inside the building the tall, polygonal, reinforced-concrete columns crowned with a gilded band give continuity to the internal space with its different events at different levels. This is also helped by the arrangement of the walls and by the unifying effect of openings on the different levels.

Outside is a staircase, a glazed »cage« of steel tubing with rectangular bronze joints. Other connecting elements have rounded, brilliantly coloured housings. In this context, the staff staircase is interesting – two parallel separate flights which provide continuity in the vertical direction. The edges are protected by brass rails. The walls are surfaced with polished green and violet Venetian hard plaster.

Across the courtyard, where Scarpa originally proposed a garden, is a roofed steel footbridge about 20 metres long, clad with curved copper-plated plywood sheets.

The extension of the Banca Popolare di Verona is an example of Scarpa's ability to introduce a new building into a historic city without historicist imitation, but rather in lively dialogue with the existing context.

Im Innern des Gebäudes gibt es polygonal geformte Säulen aus Eisenbeton mit einem weit hochgezogenen Säulenschaft. Das Kapitell ist mit einem vergoldeten Band versehen. Diese Säulen sind das regulative Element des Innenraums, der ansonsten von sehr unterschiedlichen Episoden bestimmt wird. Die Kontinuität des Raums wird dabei durch die ausbalancierte Anordnung der Wände und etageverbindende Durchbrüche gewährleistet.

Eine außengeführte Treppe ist von einem verglasten »Käfig« aus Eisenrohren mit rechteckigen Bronzegelenken umgeben. Auf andere Verbindungselemente weisen abgerundete, glänzend farbige Gehäuse hin. In diesem Zusammenhang ist die Treppe für das Personal interessant. Sie wird von zwei parallelen, aber in der Breite versetzten Läufen gebildet, die so angeordnet sind, daß sich eine Raumkontinuität in vertikaler Richtung ergibt. Die Kanten sind durch Messingleisten geschützt, die Flächen mit grünem und violettem venezianischem Stuck überzogen.

Über den Hof, für den Scarpa ursprünglich einen Garten in Halbrundform geplant hatte, führt nun ein etwa 20 Meter langer überdachter Steg, dessen Metallkonstruktion mit gekrümmten, kupferbeschichteten Sperrholzplatten verkleidet ist.

Der Erweiterungsbau der Banca Popolare di Verona ist ein herausragendes Beispiel für Scarpas Fähigkeit, ein neues Gebäude in die historische Stadtstruktur einfügen zu können, ohne imitierende Historismen, sondern in einem lebendigen Dialog mit dem jeweiligen Kontext.

A l'intérieur du bâtiment, on trouve des colonnes en forme de polygone en béton armé avec un tronc de colonne surélevé, le chapiteau est muni d'une bande dorée. Ces colonnes sont l'élément régulateur de l'intérieur qui est à part cela déterminé par diverses réalisations sur différents niveaux. La continuité de la pièce est garantie par une disposition libre des murs et des ouvertures reliant divers niveaux. Un escalier extérieur est composé d'une «cage» vitrée en tubes métalliques avec charnières en bronze rectangulaires. Des boîtiers arrondis, colorés et brillants signalent d'autres éléments de liaison. A ce propos, l'escalier réservé au personnel est intéressant. Il est en effet constitué de deux rampes parallèles, mais décalées dans la largeur, qui sont arrangées de manière à former une continuité spatiale dans la direction verticale. Les rebords sont protégés par des baguettes en laiton, les surfaces sont recouvertes de stuc vénitien poli vert et violet.

Dans la cour, pour laquelle Scarpa avait à l'origine prévu un jardin semi-circulaire, il y a maintenant un passage couvert d'une vingtaine de mètres, dont la construction métallique est revêtue de panneaux de contreplaqué courbes et recouverts de cuivre.

L'annexe de la Banca Popolare di Verona montre que Scarpa était capable d'introduire un nouveau bâtiment dans la structure urbaine historique sans historismes imitatifs, mais dans un dialogue animé avec le contexte considéré.

Staff staircase, linking the lower floors with the office levels

The elevator with its curved red wall connects the executive suite on the first floor with the second floor (above); executive suite with the customers' elevator, curtained in blue, in the background (right page)

Spiral staircase in the section connecting the new
part with the old building

CASA OTTOLENGHI

Bardolino, Verona, 1974–1979
In collaboration with: G. Tommasi, C. Maschietto,
G. Pietropoli

In 1974 a lawyer named Ottolenghi commissioned Scarpa to build him a house on Lake Garda in the village of Mure, near Bardolino. Planning regulations allowed no more than one storey above ground level. As often happens, this restriction became an important element of the architectural design. The solution was a building partly sunk into the earth and organized round nine circular columns which determine the arrangement of the rooms. The house is scarcely distinguishable from the natural surroundings in which it is half immersed. The roof became, in Scarpa's own words, »an area of rough ground which can be walked on«.

The reinforced concrete structure consists of inclined surfaces clad outside with brick and inside with polished hard plaster. The most important elements of the design are the massive columns built of discs of concrete and rough-cut stone. Scarpa wanted the stone to be cut while building was in progress, but it was not technically possible to process stone and concrete at the same time. The stone first chosen was local limestone from Prun, but it was then decided to add a few layers of Trani stone to refine the colour balance.

Thick columns are also found in other designs by Scarpa, for example for the Zoppa house at Condegliano and the cinema at Valdobbiadene, or the Roth house at Asolo, but only here did he actually build them. They function as crucial points of a polygonal organization of space, with different areas joined in an unusual way. If we were not aware that Scarpa avoided representational shapes, we could see in this project a forerunner of the compositional experiments of deconstructivism.

1974 beauftragte der Rechtsanwalt Ottolenghi Carlo Scarpa mit dem Bau eines Hauses am Gardasee, in der Gemeinde von Mure bei Bardolino. Die Bauvorschriften erlaubten nicht mehr als ein Stockwerk über der Erde. Diese Beschränkung wurde, wie es oft geschieht, zum wichtigen Gestaltungsmoment des architektonischen Entwurfs. Die Lösung war ein Gebäude, das teilweise in die Erde hineingebaut und um neun Rundpfeiler herum organisiert ist, die die Anordnung der Räume bestimmen. Es unterscheidet sich kaum von seiner natürlichen Umgebung, in die es sozusagen eingetaucht ist. Der Entwurf machte aus der Bedachung »ein Stück unebenen Geländes, auf dem man auch gehen kann«, wie Scarpa sagte.

Die Eisenbetonkonstruktion besteht aus geneigten Flächen, die außen mit Backsteinen verkleidet und innen mit poliertem Stuck überzogen sind. Wichtigstes Element des Entwurfs sind die wuchtigen Säulen aus Betonscheiben und roh behauenem Stein. Die Bearbeitung des Steins sollte, so damals Scarpas Vorstellung, während der Bauarbeiten geschehen. Es war jedoch nicht möglich, Stein und Beton gleichzeitig zu behandeln. Zunächst hatte man einen Stein aus der Region gewählt, Prunkalkstein, beschloß dann jedoch, auch einige Schichten Tranistein zu verwenden, um auf diese Weise eine raffiniertere farbliche Ausgewogenheit zu erreichen. Diese wuchtigen, dominanten Säulen findet man auch in anderen Entwürfen Scarpas, sei es für das Haus Zoppa in Condegliano, für das Kino in Valdobbiadene oder für das Haus Roth in Asolo. Doch nur hier hat er sie auch tatsächlich umgesetzt. Als Angelpunkte einer polygonalen Anordnung verbinden die Säulen die verschiedenen Bereiche, die nach ungewöhnlichen Maßen zusammengestellt sind. Wenn wir nicht wüßten, daß Scarpa die darstellenden Formen eher vermied, könnte man in diesem Entwurf einige Vorwegnahmen der kompositorischen Experimente des Dekonstruktivismus erkennen.

En 1974, l'avocat Ottolenghi chargea Carlo Scarpa de construire une maison au bord du lac de Garde, dans la commune de Mure, près de Bardolino. Les règlements sur les constructions n'autorisaient pas plus d'un étage au-dessus du sol. Cette limitation devint, comme c'est souvent le cas, le facteur créateur essentiel du projet architectonique. La solution: un bâtiment, en partie construit dans le sol et organisé autour de neuf piliers ronds qui déterminent la disposition des pièces. On ne le distingue guère des environs naturels dans lesquels il est pour ainsi dire immergé. Le projet a transformé la toiture en «un morceau de terrain inégal sur lequel il est également possible de marcher», comme disait Scarpa.

La construction en béton armé est constituée de surfaces inclinées, revêtues de briques à l'extérieur et recouvertes de stuc poli à l'intérieur. Les puissantes colonnes en rondelles de béton et en pierre équarrie sont l'élément essentiel du projet. Le dégrossissage de la pierre devait se faire, comme Scarpa l'imaginait à l'époque, pendant les travaux. Toutefois, il ne fut techniquement pas possible de travailler en même temps la pierre et le béton. On avait tout d'abord choisi une pierre de la région, une roche calcaire, mais l'on décida néanmoins d'employer aussi quelques couches de pierre de Trani, afin d'obtenir un équilibre de couleurs plus raffiné.

On trouve aussi ces puissantes colonnes dans d'autres projets de Scarpa, que ce soit la villa Zoppas à Condegliano, le cinéma de Valdobbiadene ou la villa Roth à Asolo, mais elles ont seulement été réalisées dans la villa Ottolenghi. Elles relient comme charnière d'une disposition polygonale les différents secteurs qui sont réunis selon des dimensions inhabituelles. Si nous ne savions pas que Scarpa évitait les formes figurées, nous pourrions voir dans ce projet quelques anticipations des expériences structurelles du déconstructivisme.

Passage to the living room with the blue and yellow
fireplace by Mario de Luigi (below); roofscape
with view of Lake Garda; sketch of the structural
elements (right page)

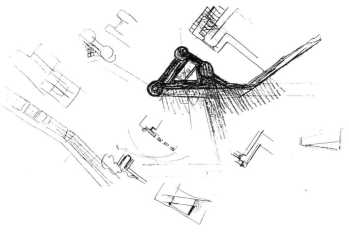

The interference between tradition and invention also inspired the idea for a concrete floor, cast and then polished, containing pieces of brick and small coloured stones to create a pattern anticipating or guiding any possible crack-lines.

The interior of the building is structured by such elements as Mario De Luigi's fireplace and the centrally situated bathroom, which serves to divide the bedroom from the large living-room. Scarpa's idea was for reflecting glass to enable those in the bathroom to see out without themselves being seen. The occupant of the bathroom feels he is in an extension of the living-room. By contrast, the interior of the bathroom is invisible from the living-room.

Auf der Interferenz von Tradition und Erfindung gründet auch die Idee für den Fußboden – bestehend aus einer Mischung aus Zementestrich und Kies, gegossen und dann geschliffen und poliert –, in den Stücke von Backsteinen und kleine farbige Steine eingelassen sind, deren Anordnung ein Muster ergibt, das eventuelle Bruchlinien schon vorwegnimmt oder ihnen den Weg vorgibt.

Von den Episoden, die den Weg im Innern des Gebäudes gliedern, sind der Kamin von Mario De Luigi und das zentral gelegene Bad besonders bemerkenswert. Es fungiert als Trennelement zwischen Schlafzimmer und dem großen Wohnraum. Reflektierendes Glas sollte es ermöglichen, so Scarpas Idee, nach draußen zu sehen, ohne gesehen zu werden. Der Raum scheint sich für denjenigen, der sich im Bad aufhält, im angrenzenden Schlafzimmer fortzusetzen.

L'idée du sol – un mélange de ciment et de gravier, coulé, puis poli – est également basée sur l'interférence de la tradition et de l'invention; il est en effet constitué par des morceaux de briques et des petites pierres de couleur, dont l'arrangement donne un motif qui anticipe d'éventuelles lignes de rupture ou leur montre le chemin.

Parmi les réalisations qui organisent le chemin à l'intérieur, on remarque la cheminée de Mario De Luigi et la salle de bains centrale. Cette dernière sert de séparation entre la chambre à coucher et la grande salle de séjour. Scarpa pensait que le verre poli devait permettre de voir à l'extérieur sans être vu. Pour celui qui se trouve dans la salle de bains, le séjour se poursuit jusque dans la chambre, et pour celui qui est dans la chambre, l'intérieur de la salle de bains demeure toutefois invisible.

ENTRANCE TO THE ARCHITECTURAL FACULTY
OF VENICE UNIVERSITY

Venice, (1966, 1972) 1985
In collaboration with: S. Los

During the restoration of the Venice architectural faculty in the Tolentini monastery, a gateway of Istrian stone was found. At first it was thought it might be used as the entrance to the faculty. When Scarpa was given the project, he did not think of this »natural« application. He wanted the gate to be used not as an entrance but displayed as a museum piece. After this had finally been decided, Scarpa brushed up the symbolic content of the gate, duplicating its allusions, and placed it in a web of cross-references, charging it with meaning as he often did with exhibits.

The old gate has become a metaphor of the entrance, quite deliberately removed from its original function. It lies in a pool of water in which steps down to the bottom form a lively underwater landscape.

The wall which was to enclose the little Campo dei Tolentini in front of the faculty was also rejected by Scarpa. The solution he proposed was to separate the structural from the architectural function. The wall encloses a small courtyard from the outside, but from the inside it almost disappears and becomes a part of the ground.

Scarpa designed three entrances, the first in 1966, the second in 1972. His last project, never completed, further developed the preceding ideas, and occupied him time and again during the last two years of his life. For the entrance construction I have relied on the second draft project, which contains a number of notes, as well as drawings intended for submission to the city council.

Während der Restaurierungsarbeiten am Tolentiner Kloster, wo die Architekturfakultät von Venedig ihren Sitz hat, wurde ein Portal aus istrischem Stein gefunden, das man zunächst als Eingang zur Fakultät einsetzen wollte. Als Scarpa mit dem Projekt betraut wurde, dachte er von vornherein nicht an eine derartig »natürliche« Verwendung. Das Portal sollte nicht in seiner Funktion als Durchgang Verwendung finden, sondern als eine Art Museumsstück ausgestellt werden. Nachdem dies grundsätzlich entschieden war, reaktivierte Scarpa den symbolischen Gehalt des Portals, vervielfältigte seine Bezüge und versetzte es in ein Spiel von Verweisen, die es mit Bedeutungen aufluden, wie er das häufig mit Werken einer Ausstellung gemacht hat.

Das alte Portal wird zu einer Metapher des Eingangs, ganz bewußt abstrahiert von der Rolle, die ihm der Funktionalismus zuweisen würde. Es liegt in einem Wasserbecken, dessen ringsum bis zum Beckengrund verlaufenden Abtreppungen eine lebendig wirkende, reliefartige Unterwasserlandschaft schaffen.

Auch die Mauer, die den kleinen Campo dei Tolentini vor dem Eingang zur Fakultät umschließen sollte, wurde von Scarpa verworfen. Die Lösung, die er vorschlug, bedeutete die Trennung der tektonischen von der architektonischen Funktion. Die Mauer umschließt einen kleinen Innenhof nach außen hin, doch von innen her verschwindet sie fast und wird einfach ein Teil des Bodens.

Für den Eingang entwickelte Scarpa drei Entwürfe, den ersten 1966, den zweiten 1972. Ein letzter Entwurf, der unvollendet blieb, entwickelte die Ideen der vorhergehenden weiter und beschäftigte Scarpa in den beiden letzten Jahren seines Lebens immer wieder. Ich habe mich bei der Ausführung auf den zweiten Entwurf gestützt, der neben Notizen eine Reihe von Zeichnungen enthält, die zur Vorlage bei der Stadt Venedig vorgesehen waren.

Pendant les travaux de restauration du cloître de Tolentini, où siège la faculté d'architecture de Venise, on a trouvé un portail en marbre d'Istrie que l'on voulait d'abord utiliser comme entrée de la faculté. Quand Carlo Scarpa fut chargé du projet, il ne songea pas dès le début à une telle utilisation «naturelle». Le portail ne devait pas être employé dans sa fonction de passage, mais être exposé comme une sorte de pièce de musée. Après que cela eut été décidé en principe, Scarpa réactiva le contenu symbolique du portail, multiplia ses rapports et le transféra dans un jeu de références, qui le chargèrent de significations, comme il l'a souvent fait avec les œuvres d'une exposition.

Le vieux portail se transforme en métaphore de l'entrée, volontairement abstrait du rôle que lui attribuerait le fonctionnalisme. Il se trouve dans un bassin dont les degrés, qui descendent jusqu'au fond, constituent un paysage sous-marin en relief vivant.

Le mur qui devait entourer le petit Campo dei Tolentini devant l'entrée de la faculté fut également rejeté par Scarpa. La solution qu'il proposa représentait la séparation de la fonction tectonique et de la fonction architectonique. Vu de l'extérieur le mur entoure une petite cour intérieure, mais vu de l'intérieur, il disparaît presque et se transforme simplement en partie du sol.

Pour l'entrée, Scarpa a élaboré trois projets, le premier en 1966, le deuxième en 1972. Le dernier projet, qui est resté inachevé, développait les idées des deux précédents et occupa sans cesse Scarpa au cours des deux dernières années de sa vie. En ce qui concerne la réalisation du projet, je me suis appuyé sur la deuxième version qui contient, outre des notes, une série de dessins destinés à la ville de Venise.

The wall to the left of the entrance contains the gate and supports a broad canopy to protect people from the rain while awaiting admission. The gate is a sort of scales in unstable equilibrium balanced on a wheel. One side consists of a heavy slab of Istrian stone bearing a quotation from Vico: »verum ipsum factum«. The other side closes the entrance with a steel-framed glass sheet. A second wheel balances the gate and adjusts its movement.

Die Mauer links vom Eingang hält das Tor und stützt ein weit auskragendes Vordach, das denjenigen, der vor dem Eingang warten muß, vor Regen schützt. Das Tor ist eine Art Waage, die sich im Ungleichgewicht befindet, aufgehängt an einem Rad. Die eine Seite besteht aus einer schweren Platte aus istrischem Stein, auf der das Vico-Zitat »verum ipsum factum« zu lesen ist; die andere Seite verschließt den Eingang mit einer stahlgefaßten Glasscheibe. Ein zweites Rad verhindert das Ungleichgewicht des Tors und reguliert seine Bewegung.

Le mur, à gauche de l'entrée, soutient la porte et supporte un avant-toit en encorbellement qui protège de la pluie ceux qui doivent attendre devant l'entrée. La porte est une sorte de balance qui se trouve en déséquilibre, suspendue à une roue. L'un des côtés est composé d'une lourde dalle en pierre d'Istrie sur laquelle on peut lire la citation de Vico «verum ipsum factum», l'autre bouche l'entrée avec une vitre dans un cadre métallique. Une seconde roue empêche que la porte ne soit déséquilibrée et règle son mouvement.

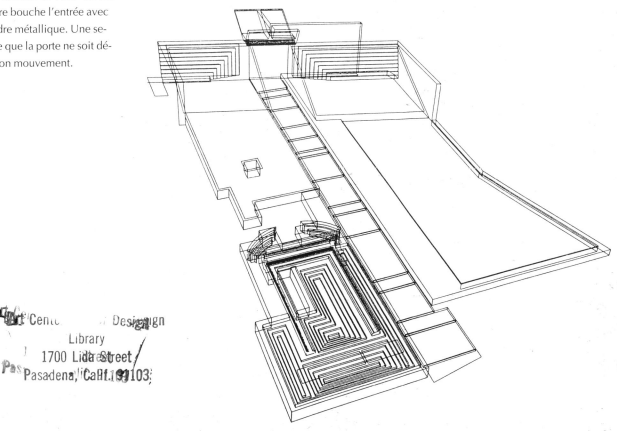

BIOGRAPHY AND EXECUTED WORK

1906 Carlo Scarpa is born on June 2 in Venice to the elementary school teacher, Antonio Scarpa and Emma Novello.
Carlo Scarpa wird am 2. Juni in Venedig geboren. Seine Eltern sind der Volksschullehrer Antonio Scarpa und Emma Novello.
Carlo Scarpa naît le 2 juin à Venise. Ses parents sont l'instituteur Antonio Scarpa et Emma Novello.

1908 The family moves to Vicenza.
Die Familie zieht nach Vicenza um.
La famille s'installe à Vicence.

1919 After the mother's death the family returns to Venice. Carlo attempts in vain to enter the Academy of Fine Art.
Nach dem Tod der Mutter kehrt die Familie nach Venedig zurück. Carlo bemüht sich vergeblich um Aufnahme in die Akademie der bildenden Künste.
Après la mort de la mère, la famille retourne à Venise. Carlo s'emploie en vain à entrer à l'académie des beaux-arts.

1920 Scarpa is accepted into the Accademia Reale di Belle Arti.
Scarpa wird in die Accademia Reale di Belle Arti aufgenommen.
Scarpa est admis à l'Accademia Reale di Belle Arti.

1922 As a student he works for two years in Vincenzo Rinaldo's architectural office.
Während seines Studiums arbeitet er zwei Jahre lang im Architekturbüro von Vincenzo Rinaldo.
Parallèlement à ses études, il travaille pendant deux ans dans le bureau de Vincenzo Rinaldo.

1924 Annex to Villa Gioacchino Velluti, Dolo, Venice

1926 Scarpa receives his diploma of architectural drawing and becomes assistant to Professor Guido Girilli at the Venice architectural faculty.
Scarpa erhält sein Diplom im Fach Architekturzeichnen und wird zunächst Assistent von Professor Guido Girilli an der Architekturfakultät von Venedig.
Scarpa obtient son diplôme dans la discipline dessin d'architecture et devient l'assistant du professeur Guido Girilli à la faculté d'architecture de Venise.

Restoration of Villa Angelo Velo in collaboration with F. Pizzuto, Fontaniva, Padua
Velo contractors' building yard in collaboration with F. Pizzuto, Fontaniva, Padua
Factory building with lodgings, in collaboration with F. Pizzuto, Fontaniva, Padua
Villa Giovanni Campagnolo in collaboration with F. Pizzuto, Fontaniva, Padua
Villa Aldo Martinati in collaboration with F. Pizzuto, Padua

1927 In addition to his teaching, Scarpa opens his own office and becomes artistic adviser to the Cappellin glass factory.
Neben seiner Lehrtätigkeit führt Scarpa ein eigenes Büro und ist bis 1930 als künstlerischer Berater für die Glasmanufaktur Cappellin tätig.
A côté de son activité d'enseignant, Scarpa a son propre bureau et travaille comme conseiller artistique pour la verrerie Cappellin.

1928 Interior of the Cappellin glassware store, Florence

1929 Interior decoration and furnishings for Vittorio Donà's house, Murano, Venice

1930 German architectural journals attract him to the structures of Ludwig Mies van der Rohe and Frank Lloyd Wright.
Durch deutsche Architekturzeitschriften wird seine Aufmerksamkeit auf die Bauten von Ludwig Mies van der Rohe und Frank Lloyd Wright gelenkt.
La lecture de revues d'architecture allemandes attire son attention sur les constructions de Ludwig Mies van der Rohe et de Frank Lloyd Wright.

1931 Rearrangement of Café Lavena, Frezzeria, Venice
Living room of the Pelzel apartment, Murano, Venice
Interior decoration and furnishings for the Ferruccio Asta apartment, Venice

1932 Rearrangement of the Sfriso silverware shop, Campo San Tomà, Venice
Collaboration with Mario De Luigi on the fresco mosaic »Il bagno«, XVIIIth Venice Biennale

1933 Scarpa becomes a lecturer at the Venice architectural faculty and begins his 14 years of work for the Venini glas factory at Murano.
Scarpa wird Lehrbeauftragter an der Architekturfakultät von Venedig. Außerdem beginnt eine über 14 Jahre andauernde Zusammenarbeit mit der Glasmanufaktur Venini in Murano.
Scarpa devient chargé de cours à la faculté d'architecture de Venise. C'est en outre le début d'une collaboration de plus de 14 ans avec la verrerie Venini à Murano.

1934 Carlo Scarpa marries Onorina Lazzari, grandaughter of the architect Vincenzo Rinaldo, for whom he worked as a student.
Carlo Scarpa heiratet Onorina Lazzari, Enkelin des Architekten Vincenzo Rinaldo, für den er während seines Studiums gearbeitet hat.
Carlo Scarpa épouse Onorina Lazzari, petite-fille de l'architecte Vincenzo Rinaldo pour lequel il avait travaillé pendant ses études.

1935 His son Tobia is born.
Sohn Tobia wird geboren.
Naissance de son fils Tobia.

Interior decoration and design for the Society of Decorative Arts of Venice

1936 Restoration and rearrangement of Ca'Foscari, Faculty of Economics, University of Venice
Interior design for the Casinó of Venice Lido
Booth for the Venini company, Murano, at the VIth Milan Triennale

1937 Installation of the »Oreficeria veneziana« exhibition, Loggetta del Sansovino, Venice, 1937
Rearrangement of the Teatro Rossini, Venice

1939 Interiors of the »Flavio« perfumery and beauty parlour, Venice Lido

1940 Tomb of Vettore Rizzo, San Michele Cemetery, Venice
Venini booth at the VIIth Milan Triennale

1941 Restoration of the Gino Sacerdoti apartment, Santa Maria del Giglio, Venice
Plan for the »Il Cavallino« art gallery, Riva degli Schiavoni, Venice
Furnishing for the Arturo Martini apartment, San Gregorio, Venice
Bedroom and dining room furniture for Gigi Scarpa, Venice

1942 Together with the artist Mario de Luigi, Scarpa accepts his first design contract for the Venice Biennale, the start of his 30 years of work for it.
Scarpa übernimmt, zusammen mit dem Künstler Mario De Luigi, erstmals einen Gestalterauftrag für die Biennale in Venedig, für die er von da an 30 Jahre tätig ist.
Pour la première fois, Scarpa est chargé, avec l'artiste Mario De Luigi, d'aménager la biennale de Venise à laquelle il collaborera pendant trente ans.

Plan and interiors for the Pellizzari apartment, Venice
Exhibit design for the »Arturo Martini« exhibition in collaboration with Mario De Luigi, central pavilion of the Biennale, Castello gardens, Venice

1943 Tomb for the Capovilla family, San Michele Cemetery, Venice

1944 Interiors for the Tessiladriatica store, Campo Santi Apostoli, Venice
Renovation of Bellotto apartment, Campo Santi Apostoli, Venice

1945 Rearrangement of the Gallerie dell'Accademia, Venice

1947 Premises of the Banca Cattolica del Veneto, Tarvisio, Udine, in collaboration with Angelo Masieri; completed by Masieri in 1949
Collaboration with Angelo Masieri on the Giacomuzzi house, Udine

1948 Exhibit designs for the XXIVth Venice Biennale, Castello gardens, Venice
Design for the »First Exhibition of Film Technique«, temporary cinema pavilion, Venice Lido
Rearrangement of the Pedrocchi Café, Padua

1949 Interior design for the new premises of »Il Cavallino« art gallery, Piscina di Frezzeria, Venice
Booth for the press and cinema advertising, temporary cinema pavilion, Venice Lido
Exhibit design for the »Giovanni Bellini« exhibition, Venice
Exhibit design for the »Rassegna d'arte contemporanea« exhibition, Alla Napoleonica, Venice

1950 Collaboration with Angelo Masieri on the Bortolotto house, Cervignano del Friuli, Udine
Arrangement of TELVE public telephone centre, Venice
Layout and furnishings for Ferdinando Ongania's antique shop, Bocca di Piazza, Venice
Interior design for the »A la piavola de Franza« clothing store, Bocca di Piazza, Venice
Book pavilion at the Biennale, Castello gardens, Venice
Exhibit designs for the XXVth Biennale, Castello gardens, Venice
Installations for the exhibition »Posters of the Biennale«, XXVth Biennale, Alla Napoleonica, Venice
Exhibit design for the »Images of Work in Contemporary Painting« exhibition, Alla Napoleonica, Venice
Installations for the »Exhibition of Cinema Books and Periodicals«, XXVth Biennale, Palazzo del Cinema, Venice Lido

1951 Scarpa meets Frank Lloyd Wright in Venice.
Scarpa lernt Frank Lloyd Wright in Venedig kennen.
Scarpa fait la connaissance de Frank Lloyd Wright à Venise.

Collaboration with Angelo Masieri on the Veritti tomb, Udine, 1951
Exhibit design for the »Giambatista Tiepolo« exhibition, Castello gardens, Venice

1952 Garden design for the Guarnieri Villa, Venice Lido
Exhibit designs for the XXVIth Biennale, Castello gardens, Venice
Exhibit design for the »Toulouse-Lautrec« exhibition, Venice
Installation of an exhibition for the Istituto Nazionale di Urbanistica conference, Ca' Giustinian, Venice
Installation of an exhibition of historical financial documents from the Commune of Siena, Marciana library, Venice
Renovation of the Ambrosini apartment, Venice

1953 Rearrangement of the historic sections of the Correr Museum, Venice
Exhibit design for the »Antonello da Messina and the Quattrocento in Sicily« exhibition, Palazzo del Municipio, Messina
Restoration of Palazzo Abatellis as the Galleria Nazionale di Sicilia, Palermo

1954 On the invitation of the Italian-American Association for Cultural Relations, Scarpa lectures in Rome; one of his subjects is museum design.
Auf Einladung der italienisch-amerikanischen Gesellschaft für kulturelle Beziehungen hält er Gastvorlesungen in Rom; eines seiner Themen: die Gestaltung von Museen.
Il donne des conférences à Rome sur l'invitation de la société italo-américaine pour les relations culturelles; l'un de ses thèmes est l'aménagement de musées.

Exhibit design for the »Arte antica cinese« exhibition, Doge's Palace, Venice
Exhibit design for the first six halls at the Uffizi gallery, Florence, in collaboration with Ignazio Gardella and Giovanni Michelucci
Venezuela pavilion at the Biennale, Castello gardens, Venice

1955 Important architects propose that Scarpa be awarded an honorary doctorate.
Namhafte Architekten schlagen vor, Scarpa den Ehrendoktortitel zuzusprechen.
Des architectes réputés proposent d'accorder le titre de docteur honoris causa à Scarpa.

Installation of L. Leoncilli's statue »La partigiana«, Castello gardens, Venice
Interior design for the Manlio Capitolo civil court, Venice
Interior design for a law office and an apartment, both for the attorney Scatturin, Venice
Interior design of the council chamber of the Amministrazione Provinciale, Parma
Rearrangement of the »Aula magna« of Ca'Foscari, University of Venice
Extension of the Gipsoteca Canoviana, Possagno, Treviso

1956 Scarpa has to defend himself in court against the accusation by the Venice Association of Architects that he is working as an architect without the necessary education or license. He is acquitted. Also in 1956, with Ludovico Quaroni he is awarded the Olivetti Prize for Architecture.
Scarpa muß sich vor Gericht gegen den Vorwurf verteidigen, er arbeite als Architekt, ohne über eine entsprechende Ausbildung und Zulassung zu verfügen. Klägerin ist die Architektenkammer von Venedig. Er wird freigesprochen. Im gleichen Jahr erhält er den Olivetti-Architekturpreis, zusammen mit Ludovico Quaroni.
Scarpa doit se défendre devant le tribunal contre l'accusation de travailler comme architecte sans disposer de la formation et de l'autorisation correspondantes. La demanderesse est la chambre des architectes de Venise. Il est acquitté. La même année, il reçoit le prix d'architecture Olivetti avec Ludovico Quaroni.

Veritti house, Udine
Collaboration with E. Detti on a parish church, Fiorenzuola
Exhibit design for the »Piet Mondrian« exhibition, Valle
Giulia modern art gallery, Rome
Restoration and exhibit design of the Castelvecchio museum,
Verona

1957   Plan for a camp site, Fusina, Venice
Design for the Taddei house, Rio Terà dei Catecumeni,
Venice
Olivetti showroom, Procuratie Vecchie, Venice
Rearrangement of the »Quadreria« at the Correr Museum,
Venice
Collaboration with E. Detti on plan for renovation of the
drawings and prints collection in the Uffizi Gallery, Florence

1958   Exhibit designs for the XXIXth Biennale, Castello gardens,
Venice
Exhibit design for the »Da Altichiero a Pisanello« exhibition,
Castelvecchio museum, Verona
Collaboration with C. Maschietto on a high school in
Chioggia, Venice

1959   Collaboration with E. Gellner on the ENI village church,
Borca di Cadore
Exhibit design for the »Vitalità nell'arte« exhibition, Palazzo
Grassi, Venice
Exhibit design for the »Vetri di Murano dal 1860 al 1960«
exhibition, Gran Guardia, Verona
Renovation of the Taddei apartment, Palazzo Morosini,
Venice

1960   Plan for the D'Ambrogio apartment, Udine
Interior arrangement of the Scatturin house, Venice
Salviati glassware showroom, Venice
Zilio tomb, Udine cemetery
Exhibit design for the »Frank Lloyd Wright« exhibition, XIIth
Triennale, Milan
Exhibit designs for the XXXth Biennale, Castello gardens,
Venice

1961   Exhibit design for the »Il senso del colore e il dominio delle
acque« exhibition in the Veneto pavilion at the Italia '61
national exhibition, Turin
Arrangement of the ground floor and courtyard of the Fondazione Querini-Stampalia, Venice
Gavina showroom, Bologna

1962   Scarpa becomes full Professor of Interior Design and moves
to Asolo, near Treviso.
Scarpa wird zum ordentlichen Professor für Innenarchitektur
ernannt und zieht nach Asolo, Treviso, um.
Scarpa est nommé professeur titulaire de décoration intérieure et s'installe à Asolo, près de Trévise.

Exhibit designs for the XXXIst Biennale, Castello gardens,
Venice
Exhibit design for the »Cima da Conegliano« exhibition,
Palazzo dei Trecento, Treviso
Interior arrangement for the Gallo house, Vicenza

1964   Restoration of the Balboni apartment, Venice
Exhibit designs for the XXXIInd Biennale, Castello gardens,
Venice
Exhibit design for the »Giacomo Manzù« exhibition, Alla
Napoleonica, Venice
Renovation of the Zentner house, Zurich

1965   In Rome, he is awarded the IN-ARCH Prize and the gold
medal for art and culture of the Ministry of Education, for his
reconstruction of the Castelvecchio Museum.
In Rom erhält er den IN-ARCH-Preis und die Goldmedaille
für Kunst und Kultur des Unterrichtsministeriums für die Neu-
gestaltung des Museums Castelvecchio.
A Rome, il reçoit le prix IN-ARCH et la médaille d'or pour
l'art et la culture du ministère de l'éducation nationale pour
le réaménagement du musée Castelvecchio.

De Benedetti-Bonaiuto house, Rome; not finished

1966   Exhibit designs for the XXXIIIrd Biennale, central pavilion,
Castello gardens, Venice
Exhibit design for the »La poesia« section at the Expo '67 in
Montreal

1967   Scarpa travels to USA to see buildings by Frank Lloyd Wright.
He meets Louis Kahn.
Scarpa reist in die USA, um sich die Bauten Frank Lloyd
Wrights anzusehen. Außerdem lernt er Louis Kahn kennen.
Scarpa se rend aux Etats-Unis pour voir les constructions de
Frank Lloyd Wright. Il fait en outre la connaissance de Louis
Kahn.

Exhibit design for the »Arturo Martini« exhibition, Santa
Caterina, Treviso

1968   Arrangement of the new Partisan Women monument by
A. Murer, Venice
Exhibit designs for the XXXIVth Biennale, central pavilion,
Castello gardens, Venice
Fondazione Masieri, Venice

1969   Exhibit design for the »Affreschi fiorentini« exhibition, Hay-
ward Gallery, London
Brion tomb, San Vito d'Altivole, Treviso
Exhibit design for the »Erich Mendelsohn drawings« exhibition, University of California, Berkeley

1970   Exhibit design for the »Giorgio Morandi« exhibition, Royal
Academy of Arts, London

1972   Scarpa becomes the head of the architectural faculty. He
moves with his office to Vicenza.
Ihm wird die Leitung der Architekturfakultät übertragen. Mit
seinem Büro zieht er nach Vicenza um.
Scarpa se voit accorder la direction de la faculté d'architecture. Avec son bureau, il s'installe à Vicence.

Exhibit design for the »Capolavori della pittura del XX sec-
olo« exhibition, Alla Napoleonica, Venice
Exhibit designs for the XXXVIth Biennale, Castello gardens,
Venice
Renovation of the Franchetti gallery, Ca'd'Oro, Venice

1973   Exhibit design for the »Le Corbusier purista e il progretto di
Pessac« exhibition, Fondazione Querini Stampalia, Venice
Banca Popolare di Verona, Verona; completed after Scarpa's
death by Arrigo Rudi

1974   Apartment block, Vicenza
Exhibit design for the »Venezia e Bisanzio« exhibition,
Doge's Palace, Venice
Exhibit design for the »Gino Rossi« exhibition, Ca'da Noal,
Treviso
Exhibit design for the »Carlo Scarpa« exhibition, Heinz Gal-
lery, London
Exhibit design for the »Carlo Scarpa« exhibition, Domus
Comestabilis, Vicenza
External renovation of the Villa Palazzetto, Monselice, Padua

Modification and extension of the San Sebastiano convent for
the new premises of the Faculty of Literature and Philosophy,
University of Venice; completed by G. Pietropoli, 1979
Ottolenghi House, Bardolino, Verona

1975 Arrangement of the »Aula magna« at the Istituto Universitario
di Architettura, Venice
Exhibit design for the »Giuseppe Samonà« exhibition,
Palazzo Grassi, Venice
Exhibit design for the »Carlo Scarpa« exhibition at the Institut
de l'Environnement, Paris

1976 Commemorative stele to the victims of the terrorist massacre
in Piazza della Loggia, Brescia
Doorway of the San Sebastiano convent, Venice

1977 Collaboration with R. Calandra on the plan of Palazzo
Chiaromonte as offices for the dean and the museum of
Palermo University
Interior design for an apartment, Montecchio, Vicenza
Exhibit design for the »Alberto Viani« exhibition, Ca'Pesaro,
Venice
Zoppi apartment, Vicenza

1978 Carlo Scarpa dies on a visit to Japan at Sendai on November
28. His will requires his burial in the Brion family burial
ground at San Vito d'Altivole. Shortly before his death, the
Venice Architectural Faculty awards him an honorary doctorate.
Am 28. November stirbt Carlo Scarpa auf einer Japanreise in
Sendai. Nach seinem Letzten Willen wird er auf dem Fami-
lienfriedhof Brion in San Vito d'Altivole beigesetzt. Kurz vor
seinem Tod verleiht ihm die Architekturfakultät von Venedig
schließlich den Ehrendoktortitel.
Carlo Scarpa meurt le 28 novembre au cours d'un voyage au
Japon, à Sendai. Selon ses dernières volontés, il est enterré
dans le cimetière de la famille Brion à San Vito d'Altivole.
Peu avant sa mort, la faculté d'architecture de Venise lui
avait accordé le titre de docteur honoris causa.

Altar and paving for the church of Torresino, Padua
Tomb for the Galli family, cemetery of Genoa Nervi; ex-
ecuted after Scarpa's death
Exhibit design for the »Carlo Scarpa« exhibition, Madrid
Exhibit design for the »Mario Cavaglieri« exhibition,
Accademia dei Concordi, Rovigo

CREDITS

The photographs by Klaus Frahm were supplemented with pictures
taken by Maria Ida Biggi, Venice (p. 26, 27), Ferran Freixa, Barcelona
(p. 82, 83), Gerald Zugmann, Vienna (p. 135), as well as drawings and
historical photos from the Archivio Carlo Scarpa, Tobia Scarpa,
Trevignano, Sergio Los, Bassano del Grappa (p. 12) and Arrigo Rudi,
Verona (p. 36, 40), the reproductions were provided by the Archivio
Tassinari/Vetta Associati, Trieste, Foto Krauss, Nuremberg, Österreichi-
sches Museum für angewandte Kunst, Vienna.